一定要學會「書信英作文」

　　「學測」英文作文開始考「書信作文」，深獲各界好評，這種作文的題型，讓全國高中學生畢業後，至少會寫英文信，非常實用。這種考試題型，在大陸的大學入學考試已經考過很多次。可以看出，「書信英作文」就是未來「學測」和「指考」的趨勢，且不容易改變。

　　針對高中同學的需要，我們特編了一本「高中書信英作文 100 篇」。我們找 15 位學校名師出題，每位出 10 個題目，發現他們重複很多，英雄所見略同，由此可知，很容易命中。我們再將題目給 100 多位高中優秀同學試寫，再由美籍老師 Christian Adams 和 Laura E. Stewart 改寫。好的英文作文，和中文作文一樣，句子要短、有力量，同學背起來又很容易。

　　由於高中同學所寫的文章，有高中同學的中文思想，有生命，貼近同學的實際情況，很容易模仿。只要背了任何一篇，立刻用得到；背 5 篇，你就會寫了；背了 10 篇，你便很會寫英文書信。這是集體努力的成果，在目錄中，每一篇都會註明命題老師、同學原文、改寫老師及翻譯老師，哪一位老師命中，他的功勞就最大。像以前，師大附中廖曄嵐老師，命中了「學測」整篇克漏字，還上了報紙頭條，大家還以為「劉毅英文」和大考中心有什麼關連！

　　「劉毅英文」的模擬試題，很多是委外命題，不同的老師命題，就會命中。今年「學測」我們就命中了書信作文的題型和內容，我們有信心，會繼續命中，團結的力量很大。

劉毅

目 錄

 建 議 (Advice and Suggestions)

> 說明： 請寫一封信給剛上高中的學弟/妹（英文名字必須假設為 Kevin 或 Julia），
> 在信中分享你（英文名字必須假設為 David 或 Lilly）自己的高中經驗以及
> 給他/她的建議。

台中女中陳虹雯老師命題；建國中學楊劭凱原文；Christian Adams 改寫；李冠勳翻譯。

> 說明： 你最好的朋友常與一群同學對班上另一不受歡迎的同學冷嘲熱諷。請你（英
> 文名字必須假設為 Jack 或 Jill）寫一封信勸他（她）（英文名字必須假設為
> Ken 或 Barbie）停止言語上的霸凌，並推己及人地幫助被欺凌的同學走出自
> 己的殼，加入班上的小家庭。

內湖高中王春仁老師命題；建國中學陳昱達原文；Laura E. Stewart 改寫；陳韻筑翻譯。

> 說明： 你最好的朋友常向你與周遭的同學借用東西，但被借的東西經常是有借無
> 還。請你（英文名字必須假設為 Jack 或 Jill）寫一封信勸他（她）（英文名字
> 必須假設為 Ken 或 Barbie）改善自己的行為。

內湖高中王春仁老師命題；建國中學葉人瑜原文；Laura E. Stewart 改寫；陳韻筑翻譯。

> 說明： 你最好的朋友喜歡網路購物及結交朋友，甚而將自己的個人資料、照片及居
> 住處毫無保留地公佈在網站上。請你（英文名字必須假設為 Jack 或 Jill）寫
> 一封信提醒他（她）（英文名字必須假設為 Ken 或 Barbie）網路世界的陷阱
> 與危險。

內湖高中王春仁老師命題；建國中學徐大均原文；Laura E. Stewart 改寫；陳韻筑翻譯。

> 說明： 你最好的朋友在垃圾分類及節省能源上的表現，真是令人搖頭。請你（英文
> 名字必須假設為 Jack 或 Jill）寫一封信提醒他（她）（英文名字必須假設為
> Ken 或 Barbie）自然資源的可貴與有限，並請他（她）為地球的永續貢獻一
> 分心力。

內湖高中王春仁老師命題；建國中學蕭承熙原文；Laura E. Stewart 改寫；謝靜芳翻譯。

6. Constructive Feedback to a Business Owner ·········· *32*
（給業者一個有建設性的意見）

> 説明： 你和家人去一家知名餐廳用餐，結果卻大失所望，發現很多缺點需要改善。
> 請寫一封信給該餐廳經理，說明失望的原因，以及改善之道。信末署名必
> 須假設爲 Daniel 或 Ella。

師大附中廖曄嵐老師命題；建國中學林上竣原文；Christian Adams 改寫；李冠勳
翻譯。

7. A Letter to My Former Self（給以前的我的一封信）·········· *34*

> 説明： 回顧至目前的人生，有沒有因爲以前某個時空曾經做過的事或做的決定而影
> 響後來的人生，讓你有所遺憾？此刻，你有個機會可以寫信給過去的自己，
> 請寫一封信給過去的你（英文名字必須假設爲 Tom 或 Sally），説服他（她）
> 改變當時的行爲或決定。

成功高中李佳軒老師命題；華江高中王盈淳原文；Christian Adams 改寫；李冠勳
翻譯。

8. Appearance Is Not Everything（外表不是一切）·········· *36*

> 説明： 你的好友最近因身材與外表問題有不少困擾，卻用不適當的方式減重，使得
> 身體越來越不健康，連帶心情也大受影響。你（英文名字必須假設爲 Chad
> 或 Cindy）打算寫一封信給你的好友（英文名字必須假設爲 Sam 或 Sandy），
> 適當地給予建議與勸告。

師大附中吳詩綺老師命題；政大附中吳之永原文；Laura E. Stewart 改寫；廖吟倫翻譯。

9. How to Learn Chinese（如何學中文）·········· *38*

> 説明： 你有個外國友人正在他們國家學習中文，但遇到學習瓶頸，因此來信向你詢
> 問如何才能學好中文。你（英文名字必須假設爲 Jacob 或 Judy）打算寫一封
> 信給你的好友（英文名字必須假設爲 Max 或 Mia），給他/她建議。

師大附中吳詩綺老師命題；北一女中何宣霖原文；Laura E. Stewart 改寫；謝靜芳
翻譯。

10. Monday Vegetarians（每週一吃素）·········· *40*

> 説明： 近日環保意識高漲，你認爲多吃蔬果少吃肉，可讓身體健康，更能降低畜牧
> 業產生的大量溫室氣體，請以 Henry 或 Helen 寫一封信建議朋友和你一起履
> 行「週一吃素日，環保救地球」。

中崙高中林淑芬老師命題；北一女中周子芸原文；Laura E. Stewart 改寫；謝靜芳翻譯。

11. **Have an Unforgettable Trip**（祝你有個難忘的旅程）⋯⋯⋯ *42*

> 說明：你最好的朋友計畫暑假花一個月騎單車環遊台灣，磨練心志，增廣見聞。請你（英文名字必須假設爲 Adam 或 Sophia）寫一封信給他/她（英文名字必須假設爲 Ben 或 Grace），給予鼓勵和提醒。

師大附中廖曄嵐老師命題；建國中學陳昱達原文；Christian Adams 改寫；謝靜芳翻譯。

12. **Getting a Friend Back on Track**（把朋友導回正軌）⋯⋯⋯ *44*

> 說明：你的朋友最近因爲社團的密集練習，導致上課期間頻打瞌睡，功課落後，與父母關係緊張。你們（英文名字必須假設爲 Tim 和 Steve）打算寫一封信給他/她（英文名字必須假設爲 John 或 Nancy），規勸他如何在社團和課業之間取得平衡。

中崙高中劉怡君老師命題；內湖高中鄭宇哲原文；Christian Adams 改寫；廖吟倫翻譯。

13. **Lost in Love**（被愛沖昏頭）⋯⋯⋯ *46*

> 說明：你的好朋友最近因談戀愛而忽略課業及朋友，你（英文名字必須假設爲 Jason 或 Judy）打算寫一封信給他/她（英文名字必須假設爲 Kevin 或 Susan），適當地給予勸告。

板橋高中林淑娟老師命題；建國中學施宇哲原文；Christian Adams 改寫；廖吟倫翻譯。

14. **Do Your Share**（要盡你的本份）⋯⋯⋯ *48*

> 說明：老師指派一項分組報告作業，在你的小組裏，有一位成員非常不負責任，幾乎沒有參與組內的分工，請你（英文名字必須假設爲 Eric 或 Cindy）寫一封信給他/她（英文名字必須假設爲 John 或 Amy），第一段告訴他組員們的感受，第二段提出你的建議或勸告。

板橋高中林淑娟老師命題；再興中學陳心謙原文；Laura E. Stewart 改寫；廖吟倫翻譯。

15. **Graduation Ceremony Suggestions** ⋯⋯⋯ *50*
（畢業典禮的建議）

> 說明：畢業典禮即將於下個月舉行，校方正廣徵意見，希望辦一個有意義且符合全體高三學生期望的典禮。你（英文名字必須假設爲 Jack 或 Jill）想寫一封信給籌劃的老師（英文名字必須假設爲 Mr. Chan 或 Ms. Chan），信中陳述你對此活動的意見與想法。

台中一中鹿梅玲老師命題；成功高中林威廷原文；Laura E. Stewart 改寫；廖吟倫翻譯。

說明：你鄰居（英文名字必須假設為 Ken 或 Barbie）養的寵物讓你覺得很困擾，請寫一封信給他，說明讓你覺得困擾的原因（英文名字必須假設為 Jack 或 Jill），並提供一些建議讓他改善現況。

板橋高中賴淑菁老師命題；建國中學劉傑生原文；Laura E. Stewart 改寫；廖吟倫翻譯。

說明：你是一面鏡子，你的主人每天總會很頻繁的使用你。請寫一封信給他（英文名字必須假設為 Ken 或 Barbie），告訴他你對他的觀感及想法。

板橋高中賴淑菁老師命題；建國中學徐大鈞原文；Christian Adams 改寫；廖吟倫翻譯。

說明：你從小學起就不斷聽到「教改」能減輕學生壓力，能讓學生有機會適性發展發揮所長。如今你已高中畢業了，個人體驗不到不斷聽到的「教改」好處，反而是第五學期結束後考學測，而且學測考試內容不含第五學期所學；第六學期結束後考指考，考試內涵蓋高中三年所有課程。你覺得壓力很大，甚至教改結果，學生們的壓力可能有增無減，而且錄取大學與否有公平疑慮。決定寫信給教育部長，抒發己見。

建國中學王星熹老師命題；內湖高中何慧瑩原文；Laura E. Stewart 改寫；謝靜芳翻譯。

說明：你（妳）是一名高中生（英文名字假設為 Harry Lee 或 Helen Lee），寫一封信給地方首長（開頭稱呼用 Dear Mayor,），針對跟你（妳）相關的公眾事務或公共建設提出建言。比方學校附近的道路路面很差，影響行車安全，希望有關單位改善施工品質；或是呼籲挽救住家附近公園的老樹等等。

北一女中唐慧莊老師命題；建國中學白善尹原文；Christian Adams 改寫；廖吟倫翻譯。

🔴 感 謝 (Thank-Yous)

說明：你剛從 Singapore 度假歸來，新加坡五日，表姊 Claude 善盡地主之誼，帶你去了夜間動物園 Night Safari，植物園 Botanic Gardens，並逛了小印度 Little India，牛車水 China Town 及烏節路 Orchard Road，並且在聖淘沙 Santosa 玩了一整天，更別提每天美食不斷。你（英文名字必須假設為 Milton 或 Monroe）打算寫一封信給她，表示感謝，並邀請她擇日來台灣一遊。

建國中學王星熹老師命題；板橋高中黃韻帆原文；Laura E. Stewart 改寫；廖吟倫翻譯。

🧑‍🤝‍🧑 道歉 (Apologies)

41. An Apology for Telling a Lie（因為說謊而道歉）……… *102*

> 說明：某一天，你對你的一個很要好的朋友說了謊（英文名字必須假設為 Ken 或
> Barbie），事隔多年，你後悔了。現在，請寫一封信給這個朋友，先解釋你
> （英文名字必須假設為 Jack 或 Jill）在什麼情況下編了什麼謊言，告訴他你
> 現在的感覺，並祈求原諒或提出要如何補償。

板橋高中賴淑菁老師命題；建國中學劉子銘原文；Laura E. Stewart 改寫；謝靜芳翻譯。

42. An Apology for an Academic Failure ……… *104*
（因為成績不好而道歉）

> 說明：你（英文名字必須假設為 Charles 或 Peggy）有一位極具耐心與愛心的英文
> 老師，尤其對你特別關心與照顧。然而，這次學校的段考你英文竟然考不及
> 格。請寫一封信，第一段說明英文不及格的原因，第二段則表達誠摯的歉意
> 並提出補救的辦法。

松山高中石坤玉老師命題；師大附中張仲豪原文；Christian Adams 改寫；謝靜芳翻譯。

☎ 問候 (Greetings)

43. Let's Stay in Touch!（保持聯絡！）……… *106*

> 說明：畢業在即，請寫一封信給校園內的任何一位人士（可以是同學、師長、或
> 行政服務同仁，但英文名字必須假設為 Bob 或 Lisa），表達你（文名字必須
> 假設為 Mark 或 Tina）的依依不捨之情，信中可以回顧過去，也可以對畢業
> 之後的雙方關係進行展望。。

成功高中李佳軒老師命題；大直高中劉玫廷原文；Christian Adams 改寫；廖吟倫翻譯。

44. Getting Back in Touch（重新取得聯繫）……… *108*

> 說明：你有一個移民國外、久未謀面的同學，最近因為網際網路的通達，又彼此聯
> 繫上。他/她很好奇你在台灣高中的學校生活、社團活動。你（英文名字必須
> 假設為 Eddie 或 Ellen）打算寫一封信給你的好友（英文名字必須假設為 Kevin
> 或 Kelly），向他/她介紹你高中生活的情況與新鮮事，並歡迎他/她有機會
> 到你的學校來玩。

師大附中吳詩綺老師命題；師大附中張景翔原文；Laura E. Stewart 改寫；廖吟倫翻譯。

45. A Letter to a Pen Pal（給筆友的一封信）……… *110*

> 說明：大學入學考試放榜了，你（英文名字必須假設為 Daniel 或 Jenny）順利考上
> 了心目中理想的大學與科系。請寫一封信，告訴一位住在美國的筆友（英文
> 名字必須假設為 Derek 或 Rose），第一段告知喜訊與你努力的經過，第二段
> 說明進入大學之後有何目標與計劃。

松山高中石坤玉老師命題；成功高中張庭豪原文；Christian Adams 改寫；李冠勳翻譯。

> 說明：你最要好的同學因病缺席多日，請你（英文名字必須假設為 Ted 或 Linda）
> 寫一封信給他/她（英文名字必須假設為 David 或 Judy），加以慰問並報告
> 學校近況。

師大附中廖曄嵐老師命題；建國中學詹士賢原文；Christian Adams 改寫；謝靜芳翻譯。

> 說明：去年暑假你到英國遊學二個月，期間住宿家庭的主人（英文名字必須假設
> 為 Mr. and Mrs. Noble）對你（英文名字必須假設為 Jack 或 Karen）非常照
> 顧及關愛，請寫一封感謝信，表達你的感激，並邀請他們有機會來台灣遊玩。

板橋高中林淑娟老師命題；松山高中林崢原文；Christian Adams 改寫；廖吟倫翻譯。

> 說明：請寫一封信給即將招待你一個月的寄宿家庭的 host mom 或 host dad（以
> Dear Host Mom, / Dear Host Dad, 開頭），介紹你自己（英文名字必須假設
> 為 Andrew 或 Anita）的家庭背景及生活習慣，並表達自己對此文化交流經
> 驗的期待。

台中女中陳虹雯老師命題；進修生賴上榆原文；Laura E. Stewart 改寫；廖吟倫翻譯。

> 說明：請寫一封信給往生過世剛滿一年的祖父或祖母（以 Dear Grandpa, / Dear
> Grandma, 開頭），表達你（英文名字必須假設為 Tony 或 Brenda）對他/她
> 的想念，以及你這一年來的改變或成長。

台中女中陳虹雯老師命題；北一女中徐寧原文；Laura E. Stewart 改寫；廖吟倫翻譯。

> 說明：請你（英文名字必須假設為 Mason 或 Mandy）寫一封信給你在國外的好朋
> 友（Logan 或 Lily），告訴他你（英文名字必須假設為 Mason 或 Mandy）
> 最近做的一件最有意義的事，並說明這件事對你生活或心情的影響。文末
> 也可以鼓勵他（她）一起讓自己的生活有意義。

中崙高中黎曉萱老師命題；新莊高中辜鈺珊原文；Christian Adams 改寫；廖吟倫
翻譯。

推薦 (Recommendations)

51. A Letter from a Fan (一封球迷寫的信) ·········· *122*

說明： 你是某位明星的忠實粉絲，最近他要成立後援會，請寫一封信給他毛遂自薦，告訴他你的愛慕之情，你想擔任什麼樣的職務，以及你為什麼認為自己可以勝任。

板橋高中賴淑菁老師命題；建國中學徐大均原文；Laura E. Stewart 改寫；謝靜芳翻譯。

52. A Movie Recommendation (電影推薦) ·········· *124*

說明： 近幾年國片復甦，優質的台灣電影，不但可以幫助振興國家的電影產業，有時更能推廣一個國家的觀光或文化。請寫一封信給你（英文名字必須假設為 David 或 Milly）的外國友人（英文名字必須假設為 Chris 或 Mary），向他推薦任何一部你曾經看過的台灣電影，並說明你推薦的原因。

成功高中李佳軒老師命題；和平高中郭孟蓁原文；Laura E. Stewart 改寫；廖吟倫翻譯。

53. A Reference Letter (一封推薦信) ·········· *126*

說明： 你的得意門生之一，近日欲申請香港中文大學（The Chinese University of Hong Kong）入學許可，希望你能寫推薦函；假設你是數學老師 Tom Smith，你的得意門生 Sean Brown 數學學測 15 級分，其餘資料請自行「杜撰」。

建國中學王星熹老師命題；陽明高中唐杰原文；Laura E. Stewart 改寫；謝靜芳翻譯。

54. A Letter to the Admissions Board ·········· *128*
（給入學委員會的一封信）

說明： 你（英文名字必須假設為 Tim Lee）即將申請某間大學校系就讀，請寫一封信介紹你自己，並陳述自己適合就讀該校系的特質。

中崙高中劉怡君老師命題；師大附中劉弘煒原文；Christian Adams 改寫；廖吟倫翻譯。

55. A Letter to a Foreign Official ·········· *130*
（給外國官員的一封信）

說明： 某國總統正在考慮是否要給予台灣免簽證的優惠。請以一個台灣人（英文名字必須假設為 Jack Lee）的身份寫封信給此位總統（英文名字必須假設為 President Smith），信中列出台灣該獲此免簽證優惠的原因。

台中一中鹿梅玲老師命題；成功高中陳亦韜原文；Christian Adams 改寫；廖吟倫翻譯。

56. A Volunteer Position（義工的職務）………… *132*

> 說明： 你想要到一家醫院擔任義工，但因名額有限，且有很多人申請。請寫一封信
> 給負責招募義工的主管（以 Dear Mr. Clement, / Dear Ms. Lee, 開頭），陳
> 述你（英文名字必須假設為 Phil Lee 或 Jill Lee）想要擔任義工的理由，並試
> 著說服他/她錄取你。

台中女中陳虹雯老師命題；景美女中魏子媛原文；Laura E. Stewart 改寫；廖吟倫翻譯。

57. Going to the Olympics（來去奧林匹克）………… *134*

> 說明： 奧運會的主辦單位正在招募國際義工。你（英文名字必須假設為 Phil Lee 或
> Jill Lee）極想獲得擔任此義工的機會。請寫一封信給主辦人（英文名字必須
> 假設為 Mr. Smith 或 Ms. Smith），信中陳述你想擔任國際義工的原因以及你
> 為何可以勝任此工作。

台中一中鹿梅玲老師命題；中山女中辛安原文；Laura E. Stewart 改寫；廖吟倫翻譯。

58. Recommending a Book（推薦一本書）………… *136*

> 說明： 你想要推薦最近你看過的一本好書給你的朋友。請你（英文名字必須假設為
> Harry 或 Ginny）寫一封信給朋友（英文名字必須假設為 Tom 或 Mary）。
> 第一段說明這本書的內容，第二段則敘述為什麼你要推薦這本書的原因。

中山女中蕭筠秀老師命題；松山高中郭韋成原文；Christian Adams 改寫；廖吟倫翻譯。

✉ 邀 請（Invitations）

59. A Most Special Volunteer（一個非常特別的志工）………… *138*

> 說明： 高中三年受到愛心媽媽 Yvonne Lee 很多照顧，諸如提供維他命、宵夜、急
> 難救助、開車送臨時有狀況同學回家等。如今即將高中畢業，同學推派你（英
> 文名字必須假設為 Zoe 或 Zara），代表三年三班寫一封信給李媽媽，表示感
> 謝並邀請她撥冗參加謝師宴。

建國中學王星熹老師命題；建國中學陳明原文；Christian Adams 改寫；李冠勳翻譯。

60. An Invitation to a Beach Party（海灘派對邀請函）………… *140*

> 說明： 二週後就是你（英文名字必須假設為 David 或 Debby）18 歲生日，父母將舉
> 辦一場生日宴會並希望你邀請同學或好友一起慶祝，請寫一封邀請函給你的
> 親朋好友。

中崙高中林淑芬老師命題；市大同高中張亦欣原文；Laura E. Stewart 改寫；廖吟倫
翻譯。

🫖 鼓勵 (Letters of Encouragement)

66. **A Letter of Condolence**（一封弔唁信）·········· *152*

> 說明：你同學的至親（父親或母親）最近因癌症過世了，他顯然受到不小的影響。
> 你（英文名字必須假設為 Jerry 或 Mary）打算寫一封信安慰他/她（英文名字
> 必須假設為 Ken 或 Anna）。

台中女中陳虹雯老師命題；建國中學陳胤竹原文；Christian Adams 改寫；李冠勳翻譯。

67. **Cheering Up a Friend**（激勵朋友）·········· *154*

> 說明：你的好友（英文名字必須假設為 Ken 或 Lucy）近日因考試成績不理想而心
> 情不佳。請以 David 或 Debby 寫一封信，邀請好友一起騎腳踏車到海邊散心。

中崙高中林淑芬老師命題；育達商職蔡文茵原文；Laura E. Stewart 改寫；謝靜芳翻譯。

68. **Hang in There**（要堅持下去）·········· *156*

> 說明：你的朋友（英文名字必須假設為 Donald 或 Betty）家中發生變故，他/她的
> 父親因工作受重傷，家庭經濟陷入困境。請你（英文名字必須假設為 Nelson
> 或 Lisa）寫一封信安慰、鼓勵他/她，並說明幫助的方法。

師大附中廖曄嵐老師命題；延平中學吳冠廷原文；Christian Adams 改寫；謝靜芳翻譯。

69. **One Door Closes, Another Opens** ·········· *158*
　　（當一扇門關上時，另一扇門會開啟）

> 說明：你的同學（Ethan 或 Emma）申請大學就讀，結果落榜。請你（英文名字必
> 須假設為 David 或 Ella）安慰他/她，請他/她不要氣餒，重新振作，把握時
> 間，和你一起努力讀書，參加大學入學考試，爭取好的成績以進入理想中的
> 大學。

中崙高中黎曉萱老師命題；北一女中簡堉明原文；Christian Adams 改寫；廖吟倫翻譯。

💙 讚美 (Compliments)

70. **A Show of Respect**（表示敬意）·········· *160*

> 說明：你（英文名字必須假設為 Jack 或 Jill）即將從高中畢業了，請寫一封信給一
> 位高中三年中，你印象深刻的班級或社團幹部，向他/她（英文名字必須假設
> 為 Ken 或 Barbie）表達謝意、敬意或歉意。

台中女中陳虹雯老師命題；延平高中吳昌蓉原文；Christian Adams 改寫；李冠勳翻譯。

71. A Letter to an Idol (給偶像的一封信) ·········· *162*

> 說明：每個人心中都有個偶像，可能是運動選手、企業家、政治人物、或是宅男女神等。請寫一封信給他/她，聊聊你（英文名字必須假設為 Charles 或 Sarah）想對他/她說的話，並寫下你對他/她最近的表現與想法。

成功高中李佳軒老師命題；士林高商汪更新原文；Laura E. Stewart 改寫；廖吟倫翻譯。

72. A Letter to the Editor (給編輯的一封信) ·········· *164*

> 說明：你/妳是一名來台灣旅遊的外籍人士（英文名字假設為 Joe 或 Jane），回國後寫一封讀者投書給台灣的英文報社（開頭稱呼用 Dear Editor,），稱讚在台灣的美好旅遊經驗，其中要包含一件令你印象深刻的特殊見聞。

北一女中唐慧莊老師命題；建國中學陳毅原文；Laura E. Stewart 改寫；廖吟倫翻譯。

🔊 抱怨 (Complaints)

73. A Complaint Letter (一封抱怨信) ·········· *166*

> 說明：最近你從 Websale 網站上買了一件洋裝，收到貨品後發現洋裝的顏色與網站圖片不一致，袖子太長且掉了一顆鈕釦。你（英文名字必須假設為 Jack Smith 或 Jill Smith）打算寫一封抱怨信給該公司，並要求換貨。

中崙高中林淑芬老師命題；中山女中蘇郁芬原文；Laura E. Stewart 改寫；廖吟倫翻譯。

74. A Letter of Complaint (一封抱怨信) ·········· *168*

> 說明：你/妳是一名消費者（英文名字必須假設為 Joe Smith 或 Jane Smith），你向一家著名的西點麵包店訂購了送朋友的生日蛋糕，但是由於某種原因（蛋糕的品質或對方的服務等）令你非常不滿意，於是事後寫信向該店抱怨（開頭稱呼語須用 Dear Sir,）。

北一女中唐慧莊老師命題；延平中學陳建銘原文；Laura E. Stewart 改寫；廖吟倫翻譯。

75. A Letter to the Mayor (給市長的一封信) ·········· *170*

> 說明：你常去高爾夫練習場（golf range）練球，總會遇到有人無視禁菸規定，在場內吸菸，球場工作人員卻視若無睹；打電話給有關當局又不得要領。你打算寫一封信 e-mail 到「市/縣長信箱」，請市/縣長督促相關人員，維護無菸環境。

建國中學王星喬老師命題；建國中學吳重玖原文；Laura E. Stewart 改寫；謝靜芳翻譯。

82. Living on Campus（住校）………… *184*

> 說明：你（英文名字必須假設為 Jack 或 Jill）的父母基於安全與方便的理由，希望你選擇家鄉附近的大學就讀，並繼續住在家中。請寫一封信給他們，信中陳述你想在大學時離家住校的原因。

台中一中鹿梅玲老師命題；林口高中柯人豪原文；Laura E. Stewart 改寫；廖吟倫翻譯。

83. The Advantages of Clubs（社團的優點）………… *186*

> 說明：你是一個熱愛社團活動的人（英文名字必須假設為 Jack 或 Jill），但你的家人和老師卻不支持你。請寫一封信給其中一個反對你玩社團的人（英文名字必須假設為 Ken 或 Barbie），告訴他你的感受，並說服他讓你繼續參與社團。

板橋高中賴淑菁老師命題；景美女中卓漢庭原文；Laura E. Stewart 改寫；廖吟倫翻譯。

84. Surfing the Net（上網的問題）………… *188*

> 說明：家中父母親嚴禁你平日使用電腦上網。請你（英文名字必須假設為 Andy 或 Annie）寫一封信給父母親，請他們放寬對網路使用的限制，說明你的課業安排，並陳述上網不會影響你課業表現的理由。

中崙高中黎曉萱老師命題；市大同高中李珮穎原文；Laura E. Stewart 改寫；謝靜芳翻譯。

85. A Study Tour in the U.S.（去美國遊學）………… *190*

> 說明：你（英文名字必須假設為 Jerry 或 Jane）想參加學校舉辦，為期三十天的美國遊學之旅。你曾經詢問媽媽的想法，但是媽媽不答應。請你寫一封信給媽媽，說明你想參加此次遊學的理由，以說服媽媽答應你的請求。

中崙高中黎曉萱老師命題；萬芳高中黃卉雯原文；Christian Adams 改寫；廖吟倫翻譯。

86. Asking for Permission（請求允許）………… *192*

> 說明：今年你（英文名字必須假設為 Billy 或 Bell）計畫和同學參加跨年演唱會，演唱會結束後會到同學家烤肉，所以當天晚上無法回家。你不敢直接口頭詢問父母的意見，所以請你寫一封信告訴或爸爸或媽媽你的計畫，並且提出具體理由說服他/她答應你的要求。

中崙高中黎曉萱老師命題；松山高中廖家琳原文；Christian Adams 改寫；廖吟倫翻譯。

詢問 (Inquiries)

> 說明： 班上要訂做班服，你在網站 Myress 上發現幾款 T-shirts 很不錯，想進一步了解團購優惠、運費、退換貨等細節，並希望能在做決定前有機會親眼見到實物。你（英文名字必須假設為 Mark Chen 或 Ellen Chen）打算透過 Myress 的「寫信給我們」功能，留一封信給 Myress，詢問相關細節。

建國中學王星熹老師命題；北一女中佐華安原文；Laura E. Stewart 改寫；廖吟倫翻譯。

> 說明： 你是一名台灣的年輕人（英文名字必須假設為 Joe Chen 或 Jane Chen），打算去澳洲（Australia）打工度假，所以你要寫一封信向承辦機構（開頭稱呼用 To Whom It May Concern:）打聽各種你想了解的相關事項。

北一女中唐慧莊老師命題；建國中學孫翌庭原文；Laura E. Stewart 改寫；廖吟倫翻譯。

要求 (Requests for Information)

> 說明： 你（英文名字必須假設為 Bill Lee 或 Sarah Lee）所參加的社團要舉辦社團發表會，但是發現經費不足，決定要寫一封信給校長，爭取經費。請在信中簡單介紹你所屬的社團以及社團發表會，並同時說明所需經費約多少，以及你們會如何使用這筆經費。

中崙高中黎曉萱老師命題；新莊高中李佳音原文；Christian Adams 改寫；廖吟倫翻譯。

婉拒 (Declining Invitations)

> 說明： 朋友熱情邀請你參加一場聖誕派對，但你（英文名字必須假設為 George 或 Mary）無法參加，請寫一封信告訴你的朋友（英文名字必須假設為 Albert 或 Tina），第一段說明你很感激對方的邀請，第二段說明你婉拒無法參加的原因。

板橋高中林淑娟老師命題；建國中學林展霆原文；Christian Adams 改寫；廖吟倫翻譯。

♠ 其他 (Others)

91. A Missed Love Connection（錯過的愛情）………… *202*

> 說明： 每天上學途中，總會遇到一個同是高三的男生/女生，你對他有好感，可惜
> 你不認識他，甚至不知道他的名字。請寫一封刊登在報紙上的公開信給他，
> 信中必須試著描述這封信的書寫對象，可以是他的外型、穿著或動作等（他
> /她才知道你在跟他/她說話），接著表達你想對他/她說的話（信末可以不
> 署名，僅描述你的特徵讓對方辨識；倘若要署名，以 John 或 May 為限）。

成功高中李佳軒老師命題；立人高中鄒蓉原文；Christian Adams 改寫；廖吟倫翻譯。

91. A Letter to an Advice Columnist ………… *204*
（寫給為讀者提供建議的專欄作家）

> 說明： 你/妳是一名高中生（英文名字必須假設為 Joe 或 Jane），你/妳寫一封信給
> 專欄作家（開頭稱呼用 Dear Lady Vivian,）訴說苦惱，例如對自己的外貌感
> 到自卑、在學校人緣不好，或是學業和課外活動無法兼顧，並請對方給你建
> 議。

北一女中唐慧莊老師命題；松山高中鄭楚玉原文；Laura E. Stewart 改寫；廖吟倫翻譯。

93. A Letter of Regret（一封表示遺憾的信）………… *206*

> 說明： 你 Mary Monroe 工作的公司 XYEL 長年捐款給「安德魯孤兒院」（Andrew
> Orphanage），但公司近日將解散，你代表公司寫信給孤兒院負責人 Milton
> Gardener 說明公司將不繼續捐款。信中客套話難免，但請節制；另可自行
> 添加相關內容，例如隨函附上數位公司員工的小額捐款若干。

建國中學王星熹老師命題；南湖高中林彥宜原文；Laura E. Stewart 改寫；謝靜芳翻譯。

94. Planning Ahead for Mom's Birthday ………… *208*
（事先規劃媽媽的生日）

> 說明： 下個星期天是你媽媽的生日，你（英文名字必須假設為 Jack 或 Jill）想以一
> 個較特別的方式為她慶生。請寫一封信給你在外地工作的哥哥或姊姊（英文
> 名字必須假設為 Ken 或 Barbie），與他/她討論慶生的細節。

台中一中鹿梅玲老師命題；松山高中陳萱原文；Christian Adams 改寫；廖吟倫翻譯。

95. I'm Innocent（我是無辜的）………… *210*

> 說明： 南韓政府現在有一條法令，支持全民當狗仔，把看到的違規行為拍下來，政府
> 再給檢舉人獎金。假設你（英文名字必須假設為 Jack Lee 或 Jill Lee）今天做
> 某件違法的事被偷拍被罰了（英文名字必須假設為 X17），請你寫一封信給
> 檢舉你的人，表達你的不滿，並為你自己的行為辯解（必須說明你做了什麼）。

板橋高中賴淑菁老師命題；北一女中許瓊方原文；Laura E. Stewart 改寫；廖吟倫翻譯。

說明：從學校畢業之後幾年，你（英文名字必須假設為 Jack 或 Jill）收到了一個同
　　　學（英文名字必須假設為 Ken 或 Barbie）寄來的喜帖，請寫一封信祝賀他即
　　　將完成人生大事。如果你會去喝喜酒，請自告奮勇為他舉辦單身派對，信中
　　　詳細說明派對的計劃跟內容。如果你不會去參加，請在信中說明為何不去。

板橋高中賴淑菁老師命題；麗山高中蔡佳伶原文；Christian Adams 改寫；廖吟倫翻譯。

說明：你（英文名字必須假設為 Jack 或 Jill）被綁架了。請利用綁匪不注意的時候寫
　　　一封信求救，信中描述綁匪樣貌或特色，自己如何被綁，以及現在情況如何。

板橋高中賴淑菁老師命題；中崙高中吳珞瑀原文；Laura E. Stewart 改寫；廖吟倫翻譯。

說明：你的老師（Miss. Lin 或 Mr. Lin）檢查作業時，誤會你抄襲別人的作業。他
　　　責備了你（英文名字必須假設為 Teddy 或 Tina），並扣你作業成績五分。
　　　請你寫一封信給老師，文分兩段，第一段說明你前一晚上花了很多時間完
　　　成作業；第二段告訴老師你對人品的重視，並請老師查明原委。

中崙高中黎曉萱老師命題；師大附中林敬富原文；Christian Adams 改寫；廖吟倫翻譯。

說明：你（英文名字必須假設為 Andy 或 Angel）參加了學校舉辦為期 20 天的環島
　　　之旅，目前人在台灣的某一個城市。請寫一封信給家人，描述旅途中令你最
印

中崙高中黎曉萱老師命題；建國中學林杰原文；Christian Adams 改寫；廖吟倫翻譯。

說明：你最好的朋友最近開始吸食毒品，眼見整個人生就要毀了，但屢勸不聽；
　　　你已經急到想舉報他了。你（英文名字必須假設為 Sean 或 Tina）知道報紙
　　　Taiwan Herald 有一專欄 Ms. Cheer，適當地給予去函讀者建議，減輕煩惱
　　　或解決問題。你（英文名字必須假設為 Phil 或 Ivy）打算寫一封信給 Ms.
　　　Cheer，訴說你的煩惱，並請教該如何幫助你的朋友。

建國中學王星熹老師命題；建國中學林上竣原文；Laura E. Stewart 改寫；廖吟倫翻譯。

 附錄（Appendix）

1. Valuable Advice to a High School Freshman from a Senior

Dear Julia,

I just heard that you're going to the best high school in Taiwan. *Allow me to say congratulations!* That's quite an achievement. You might be anxious about what to expect. Given my experience, I think I can give you some advice.

First, always know what you want, and then go for it. Don't let anything stand in your way. Life in senior high school will be colorful and it is easy to be intoxicated with it. But never lose sight of your final goal. Keep your eyes fixed on the future. Always keep moving forward. *Second, make friends.* The friends you meet during this time are important. They will be your shoulder to cry on, your light when you are in darkness.

Finally, make yourself a more complete person. Study art, music, and literature to stimulate your intellect. It will help you mature into adulthood. Julia, I know it is a long journey, but don't worry. I will be there anytime you need me. I will keep you company every step of the way.

Sincerely,
David

1. 高三生給高一新生的寶貴意見

親愛的茱麗亞：

　　我剛聽說妳即將要就讀台灣最好的高中。讓我對妳說聲恭喜！那是個了不起的成就。妳可能會很焦慮，不知道要對高中生活有什麼期待。基於我的經驗，我想我可以給妳一些建議。

　　首先，妳一定要知道自己想要什麼，然後全力以赴。別讓任何事情阻礙妳。高中生活多采多姿，很容易便沈醉其中，但絕不要忘記妳的最終目標。把妳的視線鎖定在未來，一定要持續前進。第二，要結交朋友。這時候認識的朋友很重要，在妳哭泣時，他們就是能提供妳慰藉的人。當妳在黑暗之中，他們能成為指引妳的光。

　　最後，要讓自己成為更全方位的人。要研讀藝術、音樂，和文學，這能刺激妳的智力，也能幫助妳成為一個成熟的人。茱麗亞，我知道這是個漫長的旅途，但是別擔心，當妳需要我的時候，我一定會出現。我會陪妳走過這個旅程中的每一步。

大衛　敬上

** ——————

senior〔'sinjɚ〕n. 高三學生　　achievement〔ə'tʃivmənt〕n. 成就
anxious〔'æŋkʃəs〕adj. 焦慮的　　given〔'gɪvən〕prep. 考慮到
go for it 大膽試一試；努力做　　**in one's way** 妨礙某人
intoxicated〔ɪn'tɑksə,ketɪd〕adj. 陶醉的
colorful〔'kʌlɚfəl〕adj. 多采多姿的　　**lose sight of** 忘記；忽略
fixed〔fɪkst〕adj. 固定的；（視線）不動的　　**move forward** 往前進
a shoulder to cry on 可以訴苦的人；能給予慰藉的人
complete〔kəm'plit〕adj. 全面的；完整的
literature〔'lɪtərətʃɚ〕n. 文學　　stimulate〔'stɪmjə,let〕v. 刺激
intellect〔'ɪntḷ,ɛkt〕n. 智力　　mature〔mə'tʃur〕v. 變成熟
adulthood〔ə'dʌlt,hud〕n. 成年時期　　**keep sb. company** 陪伴某人

2. A Letter Against Bullying

Dear Ken,

Classmates play an important role in every student's life. They can have a great influence on us, although we may have disagreements from time to time. *In the end,* we must be able to depend on one another for support and encouragement.

This is why it upsets me so much to see you and some of our other classmates bullying poor Sarah. You are my good friend, but when I see you do that, I feel ashamed of you. *Please put yourself in her shoes.* Imagine how she must feel with so many people picking on her and turning against her. Just like you need friends, so does she. *Moreover,* you will get nothing good from this behavior. *You may enjoy the approval of those other students for a short time, but in the end all you will feel is guilt.* As your best friend, I hope that you can stop this bullying.

Sincerely,

Jack

2. 反對霸凌的信

親愛的肯：

　　在每個學生的生活中，同學扮演著很重要的角色，而且他們可能對我們有重要的影響。雖然有時候我們可能意見不同，不過到最後，我們還是必須要彼此依賴，相互扶持勉勵。

　　這就是為什麼當我看到你和其他一些同學一起欺負可憐的莎拉時，我覺得很煩惱。你是我的好朋友，可是當我看到你這樣做，我覺得很丟臉。請你站在她的立場想一想。想像一下當這麼多人都在找她的碴和敵視她的時候，她會怎麼想。就像你需要朋友，她也需要。此外，你這種行為根本沒有好處。短時間內，你也許可以享受其他同學對你的贊同，不過到最後，你只會覺得有罪惡感而已。身為你最好的朋友，我希望你可以停止霸凌。

傑克　敬上

**

bully〔ˈbʊlɪ〕v. 霸凌　　***play a～role*** 扮演一個～角色
influence〔ˈɪnfluəns〕n. 影響
disagreement〔ˌdɪsəˈgrimənt〕v. 意見不合
depend on 依賴
encouragement〔ɪnˈkɝɪdʒmənt〕n. 鼓勵
upset〔ʌpˈsɛt〕v. 使心煩意亂
ashamed〔əˈʃemd〕adj. 感到羞愧的
put in *one's* ***shoes*** 站在（某人）的立場想一想
pick on 找…的碴　　***turn against*** 敵視；反對
approval〔əˈpruvḷ〕n. 贊成
guilt〔gɪlt〕n. 罪惡感；內疚

3.　A Letter About a Bad Habit

Dear Ken,

I need to tell you something important. *I am telling you this because you are my best friend and I care about your reputation.*

Many times I lend you my pens and erasers but you don't return them to me. *At first,* I didn't care about it or I forgot it. But then Jane told me that she had lent her eraser to you but that you had not put it back on her desk as you had promised. After this happened, I learned that many of our classmates have had the same problem with you.

I don't want to scold you, but because I am your best friend, I think I have the responsibility to tell you what others are saying. Our classmates don't trust you now, and they don't like to lend you things or even leave their things near you unattended. Maybe you think that an eraser or a pen is a small thing and that you don't need to worry about returning it. *I want to tell you that you do need to worry. I hope that you can change this bad habit.* Then our classmates may like and trust you more.

Sincerely,

Jack

3.　有關壞習慣的信

親愛的肯：

　　我必須告訴你一件很重要的事。我會告訴你，是因為你是我最好的朋友，而且我在乎你的名聲。

　　我把我的筆和橡皮擦借給你很多次，不過你都沒有還給我。一開始，我並沒有很在意，或是忘了這件事，但是後來珍就告訴我，她曾經把她的橡皮擦借給你，而你並沒有像你承諾的，把它放回她的桌上。在這件事發生後，我發現很多同學和你相處都有同樣的問題。

　　我不想罵你，不過因為我是你最好的朋友，我覺得我有責任告訴你別人是怎麼說的。我們的同學現在都不信任你了，而且他們不喜歡借你東西，或甚至把沒人看管的東西留在你附近。也許你覺得一個橡皮擦或一枝筆都只是小東西，所以你不用擔心要不要歸還。我想要告訴你，你真的必須擔心。希望你能改掉這個壞習慣，這樣我們的同學才可能會更喜歡也更信任你。

傑克　敬上

**

habit〔'hæbɪt〕*n.* 習慣

reputation〔ˌrɛpjə'teʃən〕*n.* 名聲

eraser〔ɪ'resɚ〕*n.* 橡皮擦　　return〔rɪ'tɝn〕*v.* 歸還

care about 在意　　scold〔skold〕*v.* 責罵

responsibility〔rɪˌspɑnsə'bɪlətɪ〕*n.* 責任

trust〔trʌst〕*v.* 信任

unattended〔ˌʌnə'tɛndɪd〕*adj.* 沒人看管的

4. A Letter Warning a Friend

Dear Ken,

I heard that you like to do online shopping and make friends online. *I know that you are friendly and love to make friends*. Being sociable and trusting are two of your best characteristics. *However*, it is not always good to trust others especially on the Internet.

Online shopping is really not a safe way to buy things. When you do it, your personal information might be stolen by others. You have to be very careful which websites you use and how much information you reveal. Making friends on the Internet is the same. You can't really know who you are chatting with. They may be just like they describe in their profiles, but they may not. Some people even post fake photos of themselves! *You just can't know for sure whether they are telling the truth or not*.

I know it's hard for you to be suspicious of others, but it's not always safe to trust strangers on the Internet. Please protect yourself.

Sincerely,

Jack

4. 警告朋友的信

親愛的肯：

　　我聽說你喜歡線上購物和網路交友。我知道你很友善，也喜歡交朋友。善於交際，而且容易相信別人，是你的兩大優點。然而，相信別人不一定是好事，尤其是在網路上。

　　線上購物真的不是很安全的購物方式。當你在線上購物的時候，你的個人資料也許會被他人竊取。你必須非常注意你使用的網站和你透露了多少資訊。線上交友也一樣，你無法真的知道你正在和誰聊天，他們可能真的就像他們的個人檔案所描述的一樣，也可能不是。有些人甚至會放假照片！你無法確定他們是否在說謊。

　　我知道要你去懷疑別人是一件困難的事，不過要相信在網路上的陌生人未必很安全。請保護你自己。

傑克　敬上

**

warn〔wɔrn〕v. 警告
online〔'ɑn,laɪn〕adj. 線上的　adv. 在網路上
sociable〔'soʃəbļ〕adj. 善交際的
trusting〔'trʌstɪŋ〕adj. 信任的；不懷疑人的
characteristic〔,kærəktə'rɪstɪk〕n. 特性
not always　未必；不一定
especially〔ə'spɛʃəlɪ〕adv. 尤其是
personal〔'pɝsnļ〕adj. 個人的　website〔'wɛb,saɪt〕n. 網站
reveal〔rɪ'vil〕v. 透漏　*make friends*　交朋友
chat〔tʃæt〕v. 聊天　describe〔dɪ'skraɪb〕v. 敘述
profile〔'profaɪl〕n. 人物簡介　post〔post〕v. 張貼
fake〔fek〕adj. 假的　*for sure*　確定地
suspicious〔sə'spɪʃəs〕adj. 懷疑的
stranger〔'strendʒɚ〕n. 陌生人

5. A Letter About Recycling

Dear Ken,

How is your summer vacation going? It's very hot, isn't it? You know, these crazy temperatures are a result of global warming, something that is likely to get even worse in the next few decades. But we can do something about it in our everyday life. I'm talking about recycling.

I have noticed the way you handle your trash. It is wrong! You can't just throw it out all together. *You have to divide the trash into several kinds*. If you don't, it may cause air pollution when it is burned. *In addition*, if you don't separate the recyclables, then nothing gets recycled. That is a terrible waste. *Every product we recycle helps to save resources like trees, water and energy*. These things won't last forever, you know.

I know you are a caring person who is concerned about the future. I guess you just don't realize how much of an impact your actions can have on the earth. I hope you will listen to my advice and change. If you need any information on how to recycle, just let me know. I will be happy to help!

Sincerely yours,

Jack

5. 關於資源回收的信

親愛的肯：

你的暑假過得如何？天氣很熱，不是嗎？你知道的，溫度異常的高，都是因為全球暖化造成的，這在未來的幾十年可能會變得更糟。但是關於這一點，我們在日常生活中，可以盡一份心力。我說的就是資源回收。

我有注意到你處理垃圾的方式。那是錯的！你不能把垃圾全都一起丟掉。你必須將垃圾分成好幾類。如果不這麼做，當這些垃圾被焚燒時，就會產生空氣污染。此外，如果你不將可回收的資源做分類，那就沒有東西可被回收了。這是很嚴重的浪費。我們所回收的每項產品，都有助於節省像是樹木、水，以及能源這類的資源。你知道的，這些東西無法永遠存在。

我知道你是個很體貼的人，很關心未來。我想你只是不知道，你的行為會對地球造成多大的影響。我希望你能聽我的勸告，有所改變。如果你需要如何做資源回收的資料，一定要讓我知道。我很樂意幫忙！

傑克　敬上

**

go〔go〕v. 進展　　crazy〔ˈkrezɪ〕adj. 瘋狂的；古怪的

global〔ˈglobl̩〕adj. 全球的　　*global warming* 全球暖化

decade〔ˈdɛked〕n. 十年　　*everyday life* 日常生活（= *daily life*）

recycle〔riˈsaɪkl̩〕v. 回收；再利用　　notice〔ˈnotɪs〕v. 注意到

handle〔ˈhændl̩〕v. 處理　　trash〔træʃ〕n. 垃圾（= *garbage*）

divide…into 把…分成　　separate〔ˈsɛpəˌret〕v. 把…分類

recyclable〔riˈsaɪkəbl̩〕n. 可回收的資源

terrible〔ˈtɛrəbl̩〕adj. 可怕的；嚴重的　　resource〔rɪˈsors〕n. 資源

energy〔ˈɛnɚdʒɪ〕n. 能源　　last〔læst〕v. 持續存在

caring〔ˈkɛrɪŋ〕adj. 體貼人的　　impact〔ˈɪmpækt〕n. 影響

actions〔ˈækʃənz〕n. pl. 行為　　advice〔ədˈvaɪs〕n. 勸告；建議

6. Constructive Feedback to a Business Owner

To Whom It May Concern:

Last week, my family and I dined at your restaurant. We are always looking to try another new restaurant. We liked the way your place looked, so we went inside to have dinner.

The place was crowded and the waiters seemed very busy. After a long wait, we were finally seated. Soon, we ordered the food. We waited an even longer time for the food to arrive. Frustrated, I got the attention of a waiter passing by. I asked what was going on with our meals. He went and checked with the chef. It turned out our waiter had forgotten to place our order. Rightfully angry, we left the restaurant.

Forgetting a customer's order is a big problem. If that type of thing continues, you aren't going to have any customers. *Here's a suggestion.* Require the waiters to actually write down the orders. In such a busy place, it would be impossible to remember them all.

Sincerely,
Daniel

6.　給業者一個有建設性的意見

敬啓者：

　　上星期，我家人和我在你們的餐廳用餐。我們總是在找尋嘗試新的餐廳。因爲你們餐廳的樣子讓我們很喜歡，所以我們就進去用餐了。

　　餐廳擠滿了人，所以服務生好像很忙碌。等了很久之後，我們終於坐了下來。我們很快就點好菜了。我們等上菜等得更久。因爲感到很沮喪，所以我就找了路過的服務生。我問他我們的餐點是怎麼回事。他就去跟主廚確認。結果是服務生忘了幫我們下單。我們當然感到生氣，所以就離開了餐廳。

　　忘了顧客點的菜是個很嚴重的問題。如果這樣的事情持續發生，你們就不會有任何顧客。我有一個建議。必須要求服務生確實寫下客人所點的菜。在如此忙碌的餐廳，要全部記下來是不可能的。

丹尼爾　敬上

＊＊

constructive〔kən'strʌktɪv〕*adj.* 有建設性的
feedback〔'fid,bæk〕*n.* 意見反應
To Whom It May Concern 敬啓者【用於推薦信或公開信】
dine〔daɪn〕*v.* 用餐　　place〔ples〕*n.* 餐館
crowded〔'kraʊdɪd〕*adj.* 擁擠的；客滿的
seat〔sit〕*v.* 使就坐　　frustrated〔'frʌstretɪd〕*adj.* 沮喪的
attention〔ə'tɛnʃən〕*n.* 注意　　***pass by*** 經過；路過
check〔tʃɛk〕*v.* 檢查；確認　　chef〔ʃɛf〕*n.* 主廚
turn out 結果…　　***place* one's *order*** 訂購；下單
rightfully〔'raɪtfəlɪ〕*adv.* 正當地；當然
type〔taɪp〕*n.* 類型；種類　　require〔rɪ'kwaɪr〕*v.* 要求
actually〔'æktʃʊəlɪ〕*adv.* 實際上；實際地

7. A Letter to My Former Self

Dear Sally,

How have you been? It's me. I mean, it's you. I am the person you will become in the future. Let me give you some advice. Don't look down on yourself. I know you have low self-esteem. You think you're worthless and invisible. I've got news for you, old friend. You are neither of those things. *In fact*, I'm here to tell you that great things are coming you way. *You are destined for success*.

You should surround yourself with good people who care about you. Right now, you lack self-confidence. Start feeling good about yourself. You will have phenomenal success in many areas. But you might be thinking, "How can I gain self-confidence?" *First*, you can read books. Knowledge is the key. *Knowledge is power*. Empower yourself with knowledge.

Finally, here's my last piece of advice. It's really short and sweet: speak. That's right, don't remain silent. *Speak your mind and others will respect you for it*. If you remain quiet, you will not become a better person. Keep smiling and stay courageous! I'm positive you can do it.

Sincerely,
Your Future

7.　給以前的我的一封信

親愛的莎莉：

　　妳好嗎？是我，我的意思是，也是妳。我是未來的妳，讓我給妳一些建議。不要看輕自己，我知道妳沒有自信，覺得自己沒有價值，受到忽視。老朋友，我有件事要跟妳說。妳完全不是這樣子。事實上，我是要告訴妳，就快有好事降臨到妳身上了。妳一定會成功。

　　妳應該讓好人圍繞在你身邊，也就是那些關心妳的人。現在的妳缺乏自信。要開始愛自己。妳會在許多領域有驚人的成就。但是妳可能會想：「要如何得到自信？」首先，妳可以看書，知識是關鍵。知識就是力量。知識能使妳更強大。

　　最後我有個建議。這個建議非常簡短又貼心：要把話說出來。沒錯，不要保持沈默。要說出妳心裡的話，別人會因此而尊敬妳。如果妳保持沈默，就不會成為更好的人。要保持微笑，並且要有勇氣！我相信妳可以做到。

未來的妳　敬上

**　————————————————

former（ˋfɔrmɚ）*adj.* 以前的　　advice（ədˋvaɪs）*n.* 忠告；建議
look down on 輕視；瞧不起（= *look down upon*）
self-esteem（ˌsɛlfəsˋtim）*n.* 自尊
worthless（ˋwɝθlɪs）*adj.* 沒價值的
invisible（ɪnˋvɪzəbḷ）*adj.* 看不見的；受到忽視的
have got 有　　news（njuz）*n.* 新聞；消息
destined（ˋdɛstɪnd）*adj.* 命中注定的
feel good about oneself 自愛
phenomenal（fəˋnɑmənḷ）*adj.* 驚人的；非凡的
area（ˋɛrɪə）*n.* 範圍；領域　　empower（ɪmˋpauɚ）*v.* 使有能力
silent（ˋsaɪlənt）*adj.* 沈默的　　courageous（kəˋredʒəs）*adj.* 勇敢的
positive（ˋpɑzətɪv）*adj.* 確信的

8.   Appearance Is Not Everything

Sandy,

Recently, I've heard that you broke up with a guy because of your shape and appearance. *After that*, you almost got out of control while trying to lose weight. You even tried fasting! Don't you know how unhealthy that is? I can't help but feel sorry for you. I see your health getting worse and worse. *Yet* you still force a smile every day.

I'm no expert on physical or mental health, but I want to help you. I can be a good listener. *I'm willing to listen to your troubles and to try to ease your depression*. There's a saying, "A friend in need is a friend indeed." *I will always stand by you and support you*. *Last*, remember not to injure yourself and be optimistic!

Best regards,

Chad

8. 外表不是一切

珊迪：

　　我最近聽說妳因為身材和外表的關係，和一個男生分手。之後妳幾乎失控地瘋狂減肥，甚至還嘗試禁食！妳不知道那有多不健康嗎？我不禁替妳感到難過。我看到妳的健康每況愈下，但是妳每天都還是硬擠出笑容。

　　我不是生理或心理健康的專家，但是我想幫助妳。我是一個很好的聽眾，我願意傾聽妳的困擾，幫妳減輕憂慮。俗話說：「患難見真情。」我永遠都會在妳身旁陪伴並支持妳。最後，記住別再傷害妳自己，要樂觀一點。

寄上由衷的問候，

查德

**

recently〔ˈrisn̩tlɪ〕adv. 最近　　***break up*** 分手

shape〔ʃep〕n. 身材　　appearance〔əˈpɪrəns〕n. 外表

get out of control 失控　　***lose weight*** 減肥

fast〔fæst〕v. 禁食　　***can't help but V.*** 不禁～

sorry〔ˈsɔrɪ〕adj. 難過的；遺憾的

force〔fors〕v. 勉強做出　　expert〔ˈɛkspɝt〕n. 專家

physical〔ˈfɪzɪkl̩〕adj. 身體的

mental〔ˈmɛntl̩〕adj. 心理的　　***be willing to*** 願意

trouble〔ˈtrʌbl̩〕n. 煩惱　　ease〔iz〕v. 減輕；緩和

depression〔dɪˈprɛʃən〕n. 沮喪

saying〔ˈseɪŋ〕n. 諺語　　***in need*** 在患難中

indeed〔ɪnˈdid〕adv. 真正地

injure〔ˈɪndʒɚ〕v. 傷害

optimistic〔ˌɑptəˈmɪstɪk〕adj. 樂觀的

9. How to Learn Chinese

Dear Max,

I think it's great that you want to learn Chinese! My best advice is that you visit Taiwan and spend some time here. Learning a language well requires a lot of practice. If you stayed here for a few weeks, you would have a lot of opportunities to speak it.

In addition to a lot of practice, another key to learning Chinese well is to know how to read and write the characters. I know that Chinese characters may seem very complicated. Maybe you think that it is impossible to memorize them. But don't worry. When you see a character that you are not familiar with, try to cut the many parts of the character apart. Then look the parts up in the dictionary to find out what they mean. After that, use your imagination to combine the meanings.

Chinese is really an interesting language to learn. I hope these tips will help you.

Best wishes,

Jacob

9.　如何學中文

親愛的馬克思：

　　我覺得你想要學中文真的很棒！我最好的建議就是，你得來台灣，並且在這裡住一段時間。要把語言學好，需要多練習。如果你在這裡住幾個星期，你就會有很多機會說中文。

　　除了大量練習之外，要把中文學好的另一個關鍵，就是要知道如何讀和寫中文字。我知道，中文字可能看起來很複雜。或許你認為不可能把這些字背下來，但是不用擔心，當你看到不熟悉的字時，試著將那個字拆解成很多部份，然後在字典裡查閱，弄清楚它們的意思。之後，再運用你的想像力，把那些意思結合起來。

　　中文這種語言，學起來真的很有趣。我希望這些建議能對你有幫助。

　　　　　　　　　　　　寄上由衷的祝福，
　　　　　　　　　　　　雅各

**

advice〔əd'vaɪs〕n. 建議；勸告　　require〔rɪ'kwaɪr〕v. 需要
opportunity〔,ɑpə'tjunətɪ〕n. 機會
in addition to 除了…之外（還有）　　key〔ki〕n. 關鍵
character〔'kærɪktə〕n. 文字
Chinese character 中國字　　seem〔sim〕v. 似乎
complicated〔'kɑmplə,ketɪd〕adj. 複雜的
memorize〔'mɛmə,raɪz〕v. 背誦；記憶
be familiar with 熟悉　　*cut…apart* 把…切開
look up 查閱　　*find out* 查明
imagination〔ɪ,mædʒə'neʃən〕n. 想像力
combine〔kəm'baɪn〕v. 結合　　tip〔tɪp〕n. 建議；祕訣
best wishes 由衷的祝福【信的結尾語或贈送禮物時的附加語】

10. **Monday Vegetarians**

Dear Friends,

I'm sure that you have heard about global warming. *Environmental protection is a popular topic.* Like me, you probably thought that there isn't much you can do about these problems. But I have an idea. By giving up meat once a week, we can have an impact. My idea is to become a vegetarian every Monday. I hope that you will join me.

Did you know that livestock produce methane gas? This is one of the biggest causes of global warming. *If we reduce our demand for meat, then we can reduce global warming! In addition to helping the planet, we will also be helping ourselves.* Vegetables and fruit are much healthier than meat. I hope you will agree with my plan and become a "Monday vegetarian". Let's work together and help our planet!

Best wishes,
Helen

10. 每週一吃素

親愛的朋友：

　　我相信你一定聽過全球暖化。環保是個很流行的話題。你可能跟我一樣，認為關於這些問題，我們能做的並不多。但是我有個點子，一週只要有一天不吃肉，我們就能發揮影響力。我的想法是，每週一吃素，我希望你能加入我的行列。

　　你知道家畜會產生甲烷氣體嗎？這是全球暖化最主要的原因之一。如果我們減少對肉類的需求，就能減少全球暖化！除了幫助地球之外，我們也可以幫助自己。蔬菜和水果比肉類健康多了。我希望你能同意我的計畫，成為「週一吃素的人」。我們一起努力，共同來幫助我們的地球！

寄上由衷的祝福，

海倫

**

vegetarian〔ˌvɛdʒəˈtɛrɪən〕*n.* 素食者

global〔ˈglobḷ〕*adj.* 全球的　　***global warming*** 全球暖化

give up 放棄　　meat〔mit〕*n.* 肉

impact〔ˈɪmpækt〕*n.* 影響（= *influence* = *effect*）

join〔dʒɔɪn〕*v.* 加入；和⋯一起做同樣的事

livestock〔ˈlaɪvˌstɑk〕*n.* 家畜【集合名詞】

methane〔ˈmɛθen〕*n.* 甲烷；沼氣　　***methane gas*** 甲烷氣體

cause〔kɔz〕*n.* 原因　　reduce〔rɪˈdjus〕*v.* 減少；降低

demand〔dɪˈmænd〕*n.* 需求

in addition to 除了⋯之外（還有）

planet〔ˈplænɪt〕*n.* 行星【在此指「地球」】

healthy〔ˈhɛlθɪ〕*adj.* 健康的；有益健康的

work together 合作　　***best wishes*** 由衷的祝福

11. Have an Unforgettable Trip

Dear Ben,

Summer vacation is almost here! What a relief! *Unfortunately*, I haven't made any plans yet. But I was very excited to hear about yours. Traveling around Taiwan by bicycle is a marvelous idea. *I am proud of you for tackling such a challenge*. Did you know that I did it two years ago? I'm sure you will find the experience to be very rewarding.

Here's some advice for you. *First*, make your plan as feasible and detailed as possible. Be prepared for anything. Accidents happen. *Second*, safety is the most important element of your trip. Eastern Taiwan is especially dangerous. If something should happen out there, help is often far away. *Finally*, don't take unnecessary risks. Stay on the beaten path. It's very easy to get lost in the mountains.

Well, I wish you an unforgettable trip. May God be with you. *If you have any questions, feel free to give me a call*.

Sincerely,

Sophia

11. 祝你有個難忘的旅程

親愛的班：

　　暑假就快到了！真是讓人鬆了一口氣！遺憾的是，我還沒擬定任何計畫。但是聽到你的計畫，我覺得很興奮。騎單車環台是個很棒的點子。你決定要接受這樣的挑戰，我為你感到驕傲。你知道我兩年前就做過這件事嗎？我相信你一定會覺得這樣的經驗是很值得的。

　　以下是我給你的建議。首先，擬定計畫時要愈可行，而且愈詳細越好。要為所有的事做好準備。意外是難免的。第二，安全是你這趟旅程最重要的一部分。台灣東部特別危險。如果萬一在那裡發生任何事，救援往往是來自很遠的地方。最後，不要冒不必要的風險。要待在很多人走過的路上。在山區很容易迷路。

　　嗯，我祝你有個難忘的旅程。願上帝與你同在。如果有任何問題，不要不好意思打電話給我。

蘇菲亞　敬上

** ———————————————

relief〔rɪ'lif〕n. 放心；鬆了一口氣
unfortunately〔ʌn'fɔrtʃənɪtlɪ〕adv. 不幸地；遺憾地
marvelous〔'mɑrvḷəs〕adj. 很棒的
tackle〔'tækḷ〕v. 應付；處理
challenge〔'tʃælɪndʒ〕n. 挑戰　　find〔faɪnd〕v. 覺得
rewarding〔rɪ'wɔrdɪŋ〕adj. 值得做的；有益的
feasible〔'fizəbḷ〕adj. 可實行的　　detailed〔'diteld〕adj. 詳細的
Accidents happen. 意外是難免的；天有不測風雲，人有旦夕禍福。
element〔'ɛləmənt〕n. 要素；成分　　*out there* 在外面；在那裡
help〔hɛlp〕n. 幫助；援助　　*take a risk* 冒險
beaten〔'bitṇ〕adj. 久經踐踏的；走出來的　　path〔pæθ〕n. 小徑
feel free to V. 可以隨意…　　*give sb. a call* 打電話給某人

12. Getting a Friend Back on Track

Dear John,

You've been in a bad mood lately. All your friends have noticed. *Some of us have also noticed your grades have been slipping.* In the past, you were always a top student. Ever since you joined the dance club, you have been different. Sure, it's hard to balance academics and clubs. Nobody is saying you can't do both. But you need to go about it the right way.

The first thing you should do is cut down on your practice time with the dance club. Devote more time to your studies. Dancing is fun, but your grades are your future. *Second,* take a few minutes every day to relax. You're too busy. You need to slow down. *And finally,* start getting enough sleep. Lack of sleep is probably the reason you're so crabby all the time.

Listen, John. We're your friends. We care about you. Make these adjustments in your life before serious damage occurs. None of us want to see that.

Your friends,

Tim and Steve

12. 把朋友導回正軌

親愛的約翰：

　　你最近心情不好，你的朋友都注意到了。我們有一些人還發現你的成績持續下滑。之前你一直是頂尖的學生，自從你加入了舞蹈社之後，你就變了。當然，很難在課業跟社團之間取得平衡，沒人說你無法兩者兼顧，但是你必須用正確的方式。

　　首先，你應該減少在舞蹈社的練習時間，多花一點時間在你的課業上。跳舞很有趣，但是成績是你的未來。接著，每天花幾分鐘休息。你太忙了，你的步調得放慢。最後，要有充足的睡眠，缺乏睡眠大概是你老是容易發脾氣的原因。

　　聽好，約翰，我們是你的朋友，我們很關心你。在嚴重的傷害造成之前，趕快在生活上做這些調整。我們沒有人想看到你受到傷害。

　　　　　　　　　　　　　你的朋友，
　　　　　　　　　　　　　提姆與史提夫

** ———————————————————————

get ~ back on track 將～導回正軌　　mood〔mud〕*n.* 心情
lately〔'letlɪ〕*adv.* 最近　　notice〔'notɪs〕*v.* 注意到
slip〔slɪp〕*v.* 下滑　　***in the past*** 過去
top〔tɑp〕*adj.* 頂尖的　　balance〔'bæləns〕*v.* 使平衡
academics〔͵ækə'dɛmɪks〕*n.* 學業　　***go about*** 做
cut down on 減少　　devote〔dɪ'vot〕*v.* 付出；花（時間）
lack〔læk〕*n.* 缺乏　　crabby〔'kræbɪ〕*adj.* 易怒的
adjustment〔ə'dʒʌstmənt〕*n.* 調整
damage〔'dæmɪdʒ〕*n.* 傷害　　occur〔ə'kɜ〕*v.* 發生

13. Lost in Love

Dear Kevin,

Long time no see. I called you the other night and left a message. I still haven't heard back from you. Then I went to your classroom but you weren't there. That's when I ran into Alice. She told me that you had a new girlfriend. This was definitely a shocking bit of news. I thought you would have told me about it. *However*, it explains your absence.

Love is sweet, Kevin, and I am happy for you. But don't you remember what happened with your last girlfriend? How sad and heartbroken you were when she dumped you! Well, I remember. I was the first shoulder you came to cry on. I stayed up all night listening to you cry over that girl. *And for the next several weeks, we were constant companions.* Don't forget that I was there for you then.

Of course, I wish you and your new girlfriend all the best. *I just want to remind you not to forget your friends.* We will be the ones you come crying to when this relationship fails. And they all fail, Kevin. This is high school and it's only puppy love. Remember that.

Your friend,

Jason

13. 被愛沖昏頭

親愛的凱文：

　　好久不見。我前幾天晚上打電話給你，留了言，但是沒收到你的消息。然後我就跑到你的教室，但是你不在。就在那時，我遇到艾莉絲，她跟我說你交了一個新的女朋友，這真的是一個讓我震驚的消息，我以為你會跟我說。但這也剛好解釋為什麼到處都找不到你。

　　愛是甜美的，凱文，我也替你高興，但是你難道不記得跟你前女友所發生的事嗎？她甩了你的時候，你有多傷心！嗯，我還記得。你第一個哭訴的對象就是我。我整夜沒睡，聽你因為那個女生而哭泣。接下來的幾個禮拜，我們幾乎形影不離，別忘了那時是我在陪你。

　　當然，我希望你跟你的新女友一切順利，我只是要提醒你，不要忘記你的朋友。這段感情如果結束，我們可能會是你第一個哭訴的對象。感情都會結束的，凱文。我們是高中生，這只是不成熟的戀情，要記得這一點。

你的朋友，
傑森

** ──────────────

the other night 前幾天晚上　　message（ˈmɛsɪdʒ）*n.* 留言
hear from 聽到…的消息　　*run into* 偶然遇到
definitely（ˈdɛfənɪtlɪ）*adv.* 確實地
shocking（ˈʃɑkɪŋ）*adj.* 令人震驚的
a bit of news 一則新聞；一個消息
explain（ɪkˈsplen）*v.* 解釋　　absence（ˈæbsns）*n.* 不在；缺席
heartbroken（ˈhɑrtˌbrokən）*adj.* 心碎的　　dump（dʌmp）*v.* 拋棄
cry on one's shoulder 向某人訴苦以尋求安慰
stay up 熬夜　　constant（ˈkɑnstənt）*adj.* 時常的；忠實的
companion（kəmˈpænjən）*n.* 夥伴
puppy love 初戀；少男少女短暫的愛情

14. Do Your Share

Dear John,

We do not know why you don't want to work on this project with us. Some people don't feel happy about your unwilling attitude, and they want to kick you off this team. *Needless to say,* I feel what they feel. Everyone except you knows that this project means a lot to us. As the team leader, *I'm afraid that I will have to kick you out if you don't change your attitude and work with us.*

To complete this project successfully, we must all do our share. Here are some things I want you to do. *First,* you have to apologize to your teammates, and show your willingness to work with us. *Second,* this is a "team" project, so work like a team. None of us can finish this job by himself. If you can do this, we will be happy to accept you and work together. *Otherwise,* you'll be kicked off this team.

Sincerely yours,

Eric

14. 要盡你的本份

親愛的約翰：

　　我們不知道爲什麼你不想跟我們一起做這個計畫。我們有一些人對你不情願的態度不是很滿意，他們想要把你趕出這個團隊。不用說，我也有同感。除了你以外，大家都知道這個計畫對我們很重要。身爲團隊領導人，如果你不改變你的態度，跟我們合作，恐怕我得把你趕出這個團隊。

　　爲了成功完成這個計畫，我們每個人都必須盡本份，以下有一些我想要你做到的事。首先，你必須跟你的隊友道歉，然後展現跟我們合作的意願。第二，這是一個「團隊」計畫，所以我們必須像個團隊，沒有人能靠自己完成這個工作。如果你能做到的話，我們很樂意接受你，一起合作，否則，你將會被趕出這個團隊。

　　　　　　　　　　　　　　　　　　艾瑞克　敬上

**

share〔ʃɛr〕*n.*（一人持有的）部份；（費用、工作等）分攤
do one's share 盡本份　　***work on*** 做；從事
project〔'prɑdʒɛkt〕*n.* 計畫
unwilling〔ʌn'wɪlɪŋ〕*adj.* 不願意的
attitude〔'ætə.tud〕*n.* 態度　　***needless to say*** 不用說
except〔ɪk'sɛpt〕*n.* 除了…以外
leader〔'lidɚ〕*n.* 領導者　　***kick out*** 趕走；解僱
complete〔kəm'plit〕*v.* 完成
apologize〔ə'pɑlə.dʒaɪz〕*v.* 道歉
teammate〔'tim.met〕*n.* 隊友
willingness〔'wɪlɪŋnɪs〕*n.* 意願　　***kick off*** 踢開

15. Graduation Ceremony Suggestions

Dear Ms. Chen,

I have a good plan for our graduation next month. We have studied in our school for three years, so our graduation will be very important for us. According to a study I made, most third grade students want our graduation to be held on the athletic ground. *In fact*, we are more familiar with the athletic ground than any other place in school. We have studied, run, played basketball, and even fought with our classmates there. *It is full of memories for us*. We hope we can say good-bye to our memories on it, too.

Next, most students also want the school to let all of the third grade students talk on the stage. Most students have never stood on a stage before. We hope we can talk to the audience from the stage. *It's our graduation, and we are the hosts*. These are my suggestions. I hope you can take them into consideration. Thank you very much.

Your student,

Jack

15.　畢業典禮的建議

親愛的陳老師：

　　下個月的畢業典禮我有一個不錯的計畫。我們已經在學校就讀三年了，所以畢業典禮對我們來說很重要。根據我所做的研究，大部分的高三學生都希望畢業典禮能在操場舉辦。其實和學校其他的地方比起來，操場對我們來說是最熟悉的。我們在操場唸書、跑步、打籃球，甚至跟同學打架。操場充滿了我們的回憶，我們也希望能在操場上跟我們的回憶說再見。

　　再來，大部分的學生都希望學校能讓高三學生在講台上講話。大部分的學生之前從未站上講台，我們希望能在台上跟觀眾說話。這是我們的畢業典禮，我們就是主人。以上是我的建議，希望您能納入考慮，非常感謝您。

您的學生，
傑克

**　**

graduation〔͵grædʒʊ'eʃən〕*n.* 畢業
ceremony〔'sɛrə͵monɪ〕*n.* 典禮
suggestion〔səg'dʒɛstʃən〕*n.* 建議
study〔'stʌdɪ〕*n.* 研究　　grade〔gred〕*n.* 年級
athletic〔'æθ'lɛtɪk〕*adj.* 運動的
ground〔graʊnd〕*n.* 場地　***athletic ground*** 操場
hold〔hold〕*v.* 舉辦　　familiar〔fə'mɪljɚ〕*adj.* 熟悉的
fight〔faɪt〕*v.* 打架　***be full of*** 充滿了
memory〔'mɛmərɪ〕*n.* 回憶　　stage〔stedʒ〕*n.* 講台；舞台
audience〔'ɔdɪəns〕*n.* 觀眾　　host〔host〕*n.* 主人；主持人
take~into consideration 考慮

16. A Letter to an Abused Friend

Dear Barbie,

It really bothers me to hear that your father is beating you. *Your suffering becomes my suffering.* I know you are a considerate and loyal person. To be separated from your family is almost unthinkable. *However*, staying in that situation will only cause you more harm.

I don't know if you realize how this abuse will affect your future. *The abuse is not just physical*; *your wounds are emotional as well.* Imagine some day you meet the man of your dreams but you can't accept his love. The problem is that you are afraid he might turn out to be like your father.

Frankly speaking, you need help. *First*, you must seek professional assistance. There is a counselor at our school who is very knowledgeable about these situations. Whatever you do, remember that I am here for you, and I will carry some of your burden for as long as necessary.

Your friend,

Jill

16. 給受虐朋友的一封信

親愛的芭比：

　　聽到妳爸爸會打妳眞的讓我有點生氣。妳的痛苦就是我的痛苦。我知道妳是體貼又忠心的人，妳應該無法想像跟妳家人分開，但是待在那樣的環境，只會對妳造成更多的傷害。

　　我不知道妳是否了解，受虐會對妳的未來造成什麼影響。虐待不只會造成身體上的傷害；妳的傷口也會留在心底。想像一下，如果有一天妳遇見了妳的白馬王子，但卻無法接受他的愛，問題就是妳怕他會變得跟妳爸爸一樣。

　　坦白說，妳需要幫助。首先，妳得尋求專業的協助。我們學校有個諮商師，對這種情況懂得很多。無論妳做什麼，切記有我在這裡陪妳，只要妳有需要，不論多久，我都會幫妳分擔。

妳的朋友，
吉兒

**

abuse〔ə'bjuz〕v. 虐待　　bother〔'baðə〕v. 使惱怒
beat〔bit〕v. 打　　suffering〔'sʌfrɪŋ〕n. 苦難
considerate〔kən'sɪdətɪt〕adj. 體貼的
loyal〔'lɔɪəl〕adj. 忠誠的　　separate〔'sɛpə,ret〕v. 使分開
unthinkable〔ʌn'θɪŋkəbl̩〕adj. 不能想像的
cause〔kɔz〕v. 造成　　harm〔hɑrm〕n. 傷害
realize〔'rɪə,laɪz〕v. 了解　　abuse〔ə'bjus〕n. 虐待
physical〔'fɪzɪkl̩〕adj. 身體的　　wound〔wund〕n. 傷口
emotional〔'moʃənl̩〕adj. 情緒的　　*as well* 也（= too）
turn out 結果　　frankly〔'fræŋklɪ〕adv. 坦白地
professional〔prə'fɛʃənl̩〕adj. 專業的
assistance〔ə'sɪstəns〕n. 協助
counselor〔'kaʊnslə〕n. 顧問；輔導員
knowledgeable〔'kɑlɪdʒəbl̩〕adj. 知識豐富的
carry〔'kærɪ〕v. 承擔　　burden〔'bɝdn̩〕n. 負擔

17. Please Don't Gossip

Dear Barbie,

Recently, I have heard many people speaking evil of you. *At first,* I was very angry about what they said about my best friend. I didn't know the truth until they told me that they dislike your constant gossiping. This is a very bad habit. *If you talk about other people, criticize them, and divulge their secrets, they will never trust you.* As your best friend, I would like to help you kick this annoying habit.

First, change your attitude. Try to see the best in others instead of the worst. *Remember that a shirt with a stain on it doesn't mean it is totally unclean. Secondly,* change your way of communication. The most suitable topic is something both of you can enjoy. Instead of talking about others, why don't you show interest in your listener? Ask what he or she has been doing or thinking about.

Barbie, this letter is not used to condemn you but to lend you a helping hand. I will be there if you want to discuss this with me.

Sincerely,

Jill

17.　請不要說人閒話

親愛的芭比：

　　最近我聽很多人說妳的壞話。起初我對他們這麼說我最好的朋友很生氣，但是直到他們告訴我，他們討厭妳不斷說人家閒話，我才明白事情的真相。這是一個非常不好的習慣，如果妳道人長短，批評他們，洩漏他們的秘密，那麼他們將不再信任妳。身為妳最好的朋友，我想幫妳戒掉這個惱人的壞習慣。

　　首先，要改變妳的態度，試著去看別人最好的那一面，而不是最壞的那一面。記住，有一個污點的襯衫，並不代表是完全不乾淨的。第二，改變妳的溝通方式。妳跟聊天對象最適合的話題，是兩個人都感興趣的。不要道人長短，妳何不對聽妳說話的人感興趣？問問他或她最近在做什麼，或是在想什麼。

　　芭比，這封信的用意不是要譴責妳，而是要幫助妳。如果妳想要跟我討論這件事，妳隨時都可以找我。

吉兒　敬上

**

gossip〔ˈɡɑsəp〕v. 說閒話　　recently〔ˈrisn̩tlɪ〕adv. 最近
speak evil of 說…的壞話　　dislike〔dɪsˈlaɪk〕v. 討厭
constant〔ˈkɑnstənt〕adj. 不斷的
habit〔ˈhæbɪt〕n. 習慣　　criticize〔ˈkrɪtəˌsaɪz〕v. 批評
divulge〔dəˈvʌldʒ〕v. 洩露　　kick〔kɪk〕v. 戒除
attitude〔ˈætəˌtud〕n. 態度　　***instead of*** 而不是
stain〔sten〕n. 污點　　totally〔ˈtotl̩ɪ〕adv. 完全地
communication〔kəˌmjunəˈkeʃən〕n. 溝通
suitable〔ˈsutəbl̩〕adj. 適合的　　interest〔ˈɪntrɪst〕n. 興趣
lend sb. ***a helping hand*** 幫助某人
condemn〔kənˈdɛm〕v. 譴責

18. A Balanced Life

Dear Barbie,

Everyone says that you put a lot of pressure on yourself because of your grades. This is not good for you, and it is not good for your friendships with others. I feel very sorry that some of our classmates think you care too much about your grades, and they think you are a little selfish. *Besides,* your mother also told me that you often have nightmares these days. We are both very worried about you.

I think you should take a rest for several days. Just forget your grades and stop burning the midnight oil. You are a smart girl, so relaxing a little won't hurt your grades. *In fact,* the best way to get good grades is to get enough sleep. This is just my advice. *I believe that you know what is best for you, and you will choose the best way in the end.*

Love,

Jill

18. 均衡的生活

親愛的芭比：

　　每個人都說，妳因為成績而給自己很大的壓力。這樣子對自己並不好，而且對妳的人際關係也不好。我覺得很遺憾，因為有些同學認為妳太在乎成績，而且他們認為妳有一點自私。另外，妳媽媽也跟我說，妳最近常做惡夢，我們兩個都很擔心妳。

　　我覺得妳應該休息幾天，忘掉成績的事，停止開夜車。妳是個聰明的女孩，所以放鬆幾天不會影響到妳的成績。其實，要拿到好成績，最好的方法，就是有充足的睡眠。這只是我的建議，我相信妳知道怎麼做對自己最好，而且最後妳一定會選擇對自己最有利的方式。

愛妳的，
吉兒

**

balanced (ˈbælənst) *adj.* 均衡的
pressure (ˈprɛʃə) *n.* 壓力　　***because of*** 由於
grade (gred) *n.* 成績　　sorry (ˈsɔrɪ) *adj.* 遺憾的
care about 在乎　　selfish (ˈsɛlfɪʃ) *adj.* 自私的
nightmare (ˈnaɪt,mɛr) *n.* 惡夢
these days 最近　　***be worried about*** 擔心
take a rest 休息一下
burn the midnight oil 開夜車；熬夜
in fact 事實上　　advice (ədˈvaɪs) *n.* 勸告；建議
in the end 最後

19. Looks Are Not All

Dear Ken,

How have you been? I heard from Amy that you had a nose job last week. It seems that you really care about your looks. It's important to make a good impression, but remember that being handsome is not the most important thing.

While appearance is attractive to the eye, it is character that captures the heart. It's a waste of time to focus on your looks since a person's true nobility lies in who he is and what he does. You ought to cut down on the time you spend grooming yourself. *Furthermore*, you should pay more attention to your schoolwork and never skip classes in the morning. We have the chance to improve our knowledge every day. *Unlike our looks, knowledge will last a lifetime.*

I can certainly understand why you want to look more handsome. *However*, beauty is in one's behavior, not one's mirror.

Your friend,

Jack

19. 外表並非一切

親愛的肯：

　　你最近還好嗎？我聽艾美說你上星期去做隆鼻手術。你似乎真的很在意你的外表。留下良好的印象很重要，但是你要記得，帥氣並非是最重要的事。

　　雖然外表能吸睛，但是真正能擄獲人心的是內在的品行。專注於你的外表是在浪費時間，因為一個人真正的高貴，是在於他的本質以及他的所做所為。你應該減少打扮自己的時間。此外，你應該更注意你的學校課業，早上不要翹課，我們有幸能每天增長我們的知識。不像外表，知識一輩子都在。

　　我當然能了解你想變得更帥的心態，但是美麗存在於人的行為之中，而非鏡子之中。

你的朋友，
傑克

**

looks〔luks〕*n. pl.* 外表
be not all 並非一切（*= be not everything*）
How have you been? 你最近好嗎？
nose job 鼻子整形手術　　impression〔ɪmˈprɛʃən〕*n.* 印象
handsome〔ˈhænsəm〕*adj.* 英俊的
appearance〔əˈpɪrəns〕*n.* 外表　　***be attractive to*** 吸引
character〔ˈkærɪktɚ〕*n.* 人格；品行
capture〔ˈkæptʃɚ〕*v.* 抓住　　nobility〔noˈbɪlətɪ〕*n.* 高貴
lie in 在於　　***ought to*** 應該　　***cut down on*** 減少
groom〔grum〕*v.* 修飾　　schoolwork〔ˈskul͵wɜk〕*n.* 課業
pay attention to 注意　　***skip classes*** 翹課
improve〔ɪmˈpruv〕*v.* 改善　　last〔læst〕*v.* 持續
lifetime〔ˈlaɪf͵taɪm〕*n.* 一生　　behavior〔bɪˈhevjɚ〕*n.* 行為

20. Don't Sleep in Class

Dear Nick,

I've noticed that you fall asleep from time to time in class. The college entrance exam is coming soon, and I believe that you have little time to waste. *If you want a good future, you have to stay awake and study hard.*

I heard that you play video games at night and always go out on the weekend. *In my opinion,* you can hardly afford to exhaust yourself this way. You should stop fooling around and go to bed early. Good students pay attention to the teachers. *In this way,* they make the best use of their limited time. If you concentrate in class, you can still have some free time. *You are such a smart person that you can ace the exam if you just stay awake in class!*

Love,
John

20. 別在課堂上睡覺

親愛的尼克：

　　我注意到你上課的時候爾偶會打瞌睡。大學入學考試就快到了，我想你也沒什麼時間可以浪費。如果你想要擁有美好的未來，你就得保持清醒，用功唸書。

　　我聽說你晚上打電動，週末都會出去玩。在我看來，你根本沒有本錢讓自己這麼勞累，你應該停止鬼混，早點上床睡覺。好學生上課會專心聽老師講課，如此一來，才能善用自己有限的時間。如果你上課專心，你仍舊能有一些空閒時間。你很聰明，聰明到只要上課不睡覺，考試就能考得很好！

愛你的，
約翰

＊＊ ────────────────

in class 在課堂上　　notice〔'notɪs〕*v.* 注意到
fall asleep 睡著　　***from time to time*** 偶爾
college entrance exam 大學入學考試
awake〔ə'wek〕*adj.* 醒著的　　***video game*** 電玩遊戲
in one's opinion 某人認為　　hardly〔'hɑrdlɪ〕*adv.* 幾乎不
afford〔ə'ford〕*v.* 負擔得起
exhaust〔ɪg'zɔst〕*v.* 使筋疲力竭
fool around 鬼混　　***pay attention to*** 專注於
in this way 如此一來　　***make best use of*** 善加利用
limited〔'lɪmɪtɪd〕*adj.* 有限的
concentrate〔'kɑnsṇ,tret〕*v.* 專心
free time 空閒時間　　ace〔es〕*v.* 在…方面表現得很好

21. A Noisy Dog

Dear Barbie,

It is really great to have such a nice neighbor like you. *You are always so friendly and helpful.* *However*, I think it is time for us to talk about your dog, Willy. Willy is a smart dog, and beautiful as well, but the problem is that he always barks late at night. I have a job that requires me to get up early, so I need to go to sleep fairly early. Unfortunately, Willy's barking deprives me of sleep. I'm sure the noise must bother you, too.

Here are some suggestions for how to keep him quiet and obedient. *First*, feed and walk him at a regular time. *Then* he will get into a schedule and also know when it is time to sleep. *Second*, scold him when he barks. He is such a clever dog that he will soon learn to be quiet. I hope that this advice will give both of us a peaceful night.

Yours,

Jill

21. 吵鬧的狗

親愛的芭比：

　　能有妳這樣的鄰居真好。妳總是待人友善、熱心助人。但是，我想該是時候談談妳家的狗，威利了。威利是隻聰明的狗，也長得很漂亮，但問題是牠總是在很晚的時候吠叫。我的工作需要早起，所以我很早就要上床睡覺。糟糕的是威利的叫聲讓我無法入睡。我相信妳應該也很困擾。

　　這裡有一些如何讓牠安靜聽話的建議。首先，定時餵牠，定時帶牠出去散步，那麼牠就會習慣這個時間表，而且知道什麼時候該睡覺。第二，牠如果叫的話，妳要罵牠，牠很聰明，很快就會知道要安靜。我希望這些建議可以讓我們倆都有一個寧靜的夜晚。

吉兒　敬上

** ───────────

noisy〔'nɔɪzɪ〕*adj.* 吵鬧的　　neighbor〔'nebɚ〕*n.* 鄰居
friendly〔'frɛndlɪ〕*adj.* 友善的
helpful〔'hɛlpfəl〕*adj.* 主動幫忙的　　***as well*** 也（= *too*）
bark〔bɑrk〕*v.* 吠叫　　require〔rɪ'kwaɪr〕*v.* 需要
fairly〔'fɛrlɪ〕*adv.* 相當地
unfortunately〔ʌn'fɔrtʃənɪtlɪ〕*adv.* 不幸地；遺憾地
deprive〔dɪ'praɪv〕*v.* 剝奪
deprive sb. of sth. 剝奪某人的某物　　bother〔'bɑðɚ〕*v.* 困擾
suggestion〔sə'dʒɛstʃən〕*n.* 建議
obedient〔ə'bidɪənt〕*adj.* 服從的　　feed〔fid〕*v.* 餵
walk〔wɔk〕*v.* 溜（狗）
regular〔'rɛgjəlɚ〕*adj.* 定期的；固定的　　***get into*** 習慣於
schedule〔'skɛdʒul〕*n.* 時間表　　scold〔skold〕*v.* 責罵
clever〔'klɛvɚ〕*adj.* 聰明的　　peaceful〔'pisfəl〕*adj.* 寧靜的

22. When the Mirror Talks Back

Dear Barbie,

You may be surprised to receive this letter. As your friend, there is something I need to say. Lately you haven't been yourself. Every time I see you, you seem to be so blue. *Every now and then* I hear you sigh for no good reason. I think your sadness begins with your boyfriend, Ken.

Are you worried that he might leave you? What a waste of time! As your friend, I urge you to spend your time on meaningful activities, such as reading or enjoying the outdoors. If Ken genuinely loves you, he won't leave you just because of a few pimples on your face. If he does, forget about him. Even though you are the prettiest girl in school, remember that *inner beauty counts much more than physical appearance*.

Be more confident in yourself and spend more time broadening your horizons. You are too young to be so unhappy. You have the rest of your life to look forward to. Think about the future and let the present take care of itself.

Yours truly,

The Mirror

22. 當鏡子會説話

親愛的芭比：

　　妳收到這封信可能會很驚訝，身爲妳的朋友，有些話我必須對妳說。最近妳變得越來越不像自己。每次我看到妳，妳好像都很憂鬱。偶爾我會聽到妳毫無來由地嘆氣。我想妳會心情不好是因爲妳的男朋友，肯。

　　妳擔心他會離開妳嗎？太浪費時間了！身爲妳的朋友，我建議妳把時間花在有意義的活動上，像是閲讀或是享受大自然。如果肯眞的愛妳，他不會只因爲妳臉上的幾顆青春痘而離開妳。如果他眞的這麼做，那就忘了他吧。即使妳是全校最漂亮的女孩，要記住，內在美比外在更重要。

　　要對自己更有信心，多花一點時間拓展妳的視野。妳太年輕，不該過得這麼不開心。妳的人生可以期待的還有很多。想想未來，船到橋頭自然直。

鏡子　敬上

**

lately〔'letlı〕*adv.* 最近　　blue〔'blu〕*adj.* 憂鬱的
every now and then 偶爾　　sigh〔saı〕*v.* 嘆氣
waste〔west〕*n.* 浪費　　urge〔ɜdʒ〕*v.* 力勸
meaningful〔'minıŋfəl〕*adj.* 有意義的
the outdoors 戶外；野外　　genuinely〔'dʒɛnjuɪnlı〕*adv.* 眞地
pimple〔'pımpḷ〕*n.* 青春痘　　pretty〔'prıtı〕*adj.* 漂亮的
inner〔'ınɚ〕*adj.* 內在的　　count〔kaʊnt〕*v.* 重要
physical〔'fızıkḷ〕*adj.* 身體的　　appearance〔ə'pırəns〕*n.* 外表
confident〔'kɑnfədənt〕*adj.* 有信心的
broaden one's ***horizons*** 拓展眼界　　***look forward to*** 期待
the present 目前　　***take care of*** oneself 自己處理自己的事

23. School Reform

Dear Minister,

I feel that I am a typical high school student. I would like to share my experience with you in the hope that you can better understand the concerns of the students in Taiwan.

Like many students, I enjoyed my first year in high school. I studied happily without too much pressure and even enjoyed participating in various clubs. *However*, little by little, the pressure grew. While I was a student, many educational reforms were made. I know that it was the intention to give students more ways to enter university and ease the pressure of the former JCEE. *However, the opposite is true.* My first comprehensive exam was at the end of my fifth semester. *Therefore*, I had to study for the school's tests and prepare for this important exam at the same time. It was difficult to know which to give priority because both good grades and good exam scores are necessary to enter university. Now I am faced with the same dilemma as I prepare for another large exam at the end of my sixth semester.

I hope you will reconsider this educational policy. High school students in Taiwan should focus on learning, not on simply passing exams.

Yours sincerely,
Stephen Lee

23. 教 改

親愛的部長：

　　我覺得我是個典型的高中生。我想要和您分享我的經驗，希望您能更了解台灣學生所關心的事。

　　就像許多學生一樣，我很喜歡高一生活，我唸書唸得很愉快，並沒有太多的壓力，甚至很喜歡參加各式各樣的社團。不過，漸漸地，壓力變大了。當我是個學生時，進行了許多教育改革，我知道教改的目的是要讓學生有更多方式進入大學，並減少以前聯考的壓力。但是，正好相反。我的第一次大考是在高三上學期結束時。因此，我必須應付學校考試，同時又準備這場重要的考試。很難判斷何者優先，因為良好的在校成績和優秀的大考成績，都是上大學必備的條件。現在當我在準備高三下學期結束時的另一場大考時，也面臨同樣兩難的情況。

　　我希望您能再考慮一下這個教育政策。台灣的高中生應該專注於學習，而不只是致力於通過考試。

史蒂芬‧李　敬上

**　

school〔skul〕*n.* 學校教育　　reform〔rɪ'fɔrm〕*n.* 改革
minister〔'mɪnɪstə〕*n.* 部長　　typical〔'tɪpɪkḷ〕*adj.* 典型的
in the hope that 希望　　concern〔kən'sɝn〕*n.* 關心的事
participate in 參加　　club〔klʌb〕*n.* 社團
little by little 漸漸地　　grow〔gro〕*v.* 增大
intention〔ɪn'tɛnʃən〕*n.* 用意　　ease〔iz〕*v.* 減輕；緩和
former〔'fɔrmə〕*adj.* 以前的
JCEE 大學聯考（= *Joint College Entrance Exam*）
The opposite is true. 正好相反。
comprehensive〔ˌkɑmprɪ'hɛnsɪv〕*adj.* 全面的；綜合性的
priority〔praɪ'ɔrətɪ〕*n.* 優先　　***be faced with*** 面對
dilemma〔də'lɛmə〕*n.* 進退兩難；左右為難
reconsider〔ˌrikən'sɪdə〕*v.* 再考慮　　***focus on*** 專注於

24. A Letter to the Mayor

Dear Mayor,

My name is Harry Lee and I am a senior high school student. *First*, I want to thank you for all the things you have done for our city. I really appreciate that. *But there are still some areas with room for improvement*.

The first area is the trash problem. Pollution is everywhere in this city. *Also*, there is a problem with trash collection. People frequently miss the trash trucks. I suggest that the government designate a place for people to throw their trash. It would solve the problem of failing to catch the trash trucks. *Besides*, the roads in the city are in bad shape. The conditions contribute to traffic accidents. *Because it involves public safety, of all the problems, this is the most urgent*.

Certainly there are still many small problems to deal with. I hope that the government can listen to the citizens more and ask their opinions. Thanks a lot for reading this letter.

Sincerely,

Harry Lee

24. 給市長的一封信

親愛的市長：

　　我的名字叫作李亨利，我是個高中生。首先，我想要感謝您爲我們的城市所做的一切，我眞的很感激，但是仍然有一些需要改善的地方。

　　第一個部分是垃圾的問題。市區到處都是污染，收垃圾也有問題，市民經常錯過垃圾車。我建議政府指定一個地方讓大家丟垃圾，這可以解決趕不上垃圾車的問題。此外，市區的道路狀況不佳，這會造成很多車禍，因爲這牽涉到大衆安全的問題，所以在所有的問題之中，這個是最迫切的。

　　當然還是有很多需要處理的小問題，我希望政府可以多傾聽小市民的心聲，並詢問他們的意見。謝謝您撥空看這封信。

　　　　　　　　　　　　　　　　李亨利　敬上

** ─────────────────────

mayor (ˈmeɚ) *n.* 市長　　appreciate (əˈpriʃɪˌet) *v.* 感激
area (ˈɛrɪə) *n.* 地區；領域　　room (rum) *n.* 空間
improvement (ɪmˈpruvmənt) *n.* 改善
pollution (pəˈluʃən) *n.* 汙染　　collection (kəˈlɛkʃən) *n.* 收集
frequently (ˈfrikwəntlɪ) *adv.* 經常　　miss (mɪs) *v.* 錯過
trash truck 垃圾車　　government (ˈgʌvənmənt) *n.* 政府
designate (ˈdɛzɪgˌnet) *v.* 指定　　**fail to V.** 無法～
catch (kætʃ) *v.* 趕上　　**be in bad shape** 狀況不佳
condition (kənˈdɪʃən) *n.* 狀況　　**contribute to** 導致；造成
involve (ɪnˈvɑlv) *v.* 牽涉
public (ˈpʌblɪk) *adj.* 大衆的；公共的
urgent (ˈɝdʒənt) *adj.* 迫切的　　**deal with** 應付；處理
citizen (ˈsɪtəzn̩) *n.* 市民

25. Thank You for the Hospitality

Dear Claude,

I just arrived home, but I can't wait to write to you. It is hard to believe that I'm already back in Taiwan. *Thanks to your hospitality, the days in Singapore were so full of fun and excitement that they just flew by.* There was never a dull moment. I can still remember all the fascinating things I saw. But eating out with you was the most eye-opening experience. You took me to some wonderful places. The food in Little India, Chinatown and Orchard Road was as delicious as could be. I still can't believe that you get to eat like this every day! But as you may know, the food in Taiwan is also remarkable. I can't wait to introduce it to you. I bet you'll love it.

I really hope that you will visit me as soon as possible. *I would like to have the chance show you the delights of Taiwan and to treat you as well as you have treated me.* I really appreciate your hospitality and companionship (not to mention the food), so let me urge you again: be my guest!

Lots of love,

Monroe

25. 感謝招待

親愛的克勞德：

　　我剛到家，可是我已經等不及要寫信給你了。很難相信我已經回到台灣。因為你的熱情款待，我在新加坡的這幾天充滿了樂趣及興奮，所以時間過得特別快。完全沒有無聊的時候。我仍然記得我看過的所有迷人的事物。但外出跟你用餐是最讓我大開眼界的經驗。你帶我去一些很棒的餐廳，小印度，中國城，以及烏節路的美食，真是美味至極。我真不敢相信，你每天都可以享用這樣的美食！但是你也知道，台灣的美食也是很棒的，我等不及要介紹給你了。我打包票你一定會喜歡。

　　我真的很希望你能儘快來拜訪我。我很想要有機會帶你去體驗台灣之美，像你招待我一樣的招待你。我很感謝你的熱情招待以及友誼（更不用說食物了），所以我要再催促你一次：來當我的客人！

門羅 敬上

**

hospitality〔ˌhɑspɪˈtælətɪ〕*n.* 慇懃招待；款待
thanks to 因為；由於　　***fly by*** （時光）飛逝
dull〔dʌl〕*adj.* 無聊的
fascinating〔ˈfæsṇˌetɪŋ〕*adj.* 迷人的　　***eat out*** 外出用餐
eye-opening *adj.* 大開眼界的　　place〔ples〕*n.* 餐館
a s…as can be 非常…　　***get to V.*** 得以…
remarkable〔rɪˈmɑrkəbḷ〕*adj.* 驚人的；出色的
bet〔bɛt〕*v.* 打賭；猜想　　***as soon as possible*** 儘快
delight〔dɪˈlaɪt〕*n.* 令人高興的事；樂事；樂趣
appreciate〔əˈpriʃɪˌet〕*v.* 感激
companionship〔kəmˈpænjənˌʃɪp〕*n.* 友誼
urge〔ɝdʒ〕*v.* 催促；力勸　　***not to mention*** 更別提

26.　To the Most Supportive Teacher

Dear Teacher,

I have great news! I was just accepted to my ideal college. Wait, there's more. I was also admitted into my ideal department! Without you, this would have been impossible. *I can't thank you enough*. You were always patient with me. You spared no effort to help me solve my problems. Were it not for your encouragement, I wouldn't have been able to improve my English, let alone enter such a famous university!

In college, I plan to continue polishing my English skills. If time permits, I will learn another foreign language. By doing so, I can be more competitive in this global society. *Moreover, I will follow in your footsteps*. My goal is to help other people, just as you have done for me.

Again, you have my deepest gratitude. It is my pleasure to share this good news. It is your achievement, too. I could not have been successful without you. *One day, I hope to make you proud*.

Sincerely,
Lisa

26. 給最支持我的老師

親愛的老師：

　　我有個好消息！我剛被我理想的大學錄取。等一下，不只是這樣，我也獲准進入我理想的科系！沒有您，這一切都不可能發生。我對您感激不盡。您總是對我很有耐心，不遺餘力地幫助我解決問題。要不是您的鼓勵，我無法增進我的英文能力，更不用說進入一所著名的大學了。

　　在大學裡，我打算要增進我的英文能力。如果時間允許，我會學另一個外語。如此一來，我可以在這全球性的社會更有競爭力。此外，我會跟隨您的腳步。我的目標是幫助其他人，就如同您為我所做的一樣。

　　我要再次向您表達最深的感謝。可以跟您分享這個好消息是我的榮幸，這也是您的成就。沒有您，我無法成功。我希望將來有一天，我能讓您引以為榮。

麗莎　敬上

** ————————————

supportive〔sə'portɪv〕*adj.* 給予幫助的；支持的
accept〔ək'sɛpt〕*v.* 接受　　admit〔əd'mɪt〕*v.* 准許（進入）
department〔dɪ'partmənt〕*n.*（大學的）科系
can't + V. enough 非常…　　patient〔'peʃənt〕*adj.* 有耐心的
spare〔spɛr〕*v.* 吝惜；節省　　***spare no effort*** 不遺餘力
solve〔salv〕*v.* 解決　　***were it not for*** 如果沒有；要不是
encouragement〔ɪn'kɝɪdʒmənt〕*n.* 鼓勵
let alone 更不用說　　polish〔'palɪʃ〕*v.* 增強
if time permits 如果時間允許
competitive〔kəm'pɛtətɪv〕*adj.* 有競爭力的
global〔'globḷ〕*adj.* 全球的
follow in *one's* ***footsteps*** 跟隨某人的腳步；效法某人
gratitude〔'grætə,tjud〕*n.* 感謝　　pleasure〔'plɛʒɚ〕*n.* 榮幸
achievement〔ə'tʃivmənt〕*n.* 成就

27. A Good Taxi Driver

Dear Editor,

I am a native of China and I work in Taipei now. Taiwan is wonderful, and so are its residents. People in Taiwan are very kind. Wherever I go, I see people helping one another. *Joyfully*, I experienced that last night.

I was working hard at my computer on an important project that my boss wanted me to do as soon as possible. I was so concentrated on my work that I forgot about my son's music performance at 7:00. At a quarter to seven, my cell phone rang. It was my son. I grabbed my jacket quickly, ran out of my office and rushed into a taxi. I was very nervous and told the driver to drive as fast as possible. But then I realized that I hadn't taken any money with me when I left the office! I told the taxi driver and asked him to return to my office. *Surprisingly*, *that driver smiled at me and told me that my concern for my son made him think of his son*, *who was also in elementary school*. He would drive me for free and help me be on time to see my son!

I don't know the driver's name, but I'm very, very grateful to him. I think Taiwan is a beautiful and warm island.

Sincerely,

Joe Wang

27.　一位善良的計程車司機

親愛的編輯：

　　我是在台北工作的中國人。台灣很棒，台灣的居民也很好。台灣人很善良，不管走到哪，都可以看到大家互相幫忙，我很高興昨晚我就能感受到這善良的一面。

　　昨天我在電腦前努力工作，想要快點完成老闆交代的重要專案。我太專注於工作，所以忘了我兒子七點的音樂表演。六點四十五分的時候，我的手機響了，是我兒子打來的。我很快抓了夾克，衝出辦公室，鑽進一輛計程車裡。我很緊張，而且叫司機開快點。然後那時我才發現，我離開辦公室的時候忘記帶錢！我告訴司機我沒帶錢，要他開回我的辦公室。令我驚訝的是，司機笑著跟我說，我對兒子的關心讓他想到他也在讀小學的兒子，他願意免費載我一程，幫助我準時看到我兒子的演出！

　　我不知道那位司機的名字，但是我非常、非常感激他，我覺得台灣是個美麗又窩心的島嶼。

王喬　敬上

** ────────────

native〔ˈnetɪv〕n. 本國人；本地人
resident〔ˈrɛzədənt〕n. 居民　　joyfully〔ˈdʒɔɪfəlɪ〕adv. 愉快地
project〔ˈprɑdʒɛkt〕n. 計劃；專案
concentrated〔ˈkɑnsɛnˌtretɪd〕adj. 專心的
performance〔pəˈfɔrməns〕n. 表演
quarter〔ˈkɔrtɚ〕n. 十五分鐘
a quarter to seven 差十五分鐘七點；六點四十五分
grab〔græb〕v. 抓住　　rush〔rʌʃ〕v. 衝
nervous〔ˈnɜvəs〕adj. 緊張的　　realize〔ˈriəˌlaɪz〕v. 了解
concern〔kənˈsɜn〕n. 關心；擔心　　*drive sb.* 開車載某人
for free 免費地　　*on time* 準時
grateful〔ˈgretfəl〕adj. 感激的

28. **Thanking a Friend**

Dear Sandy,

Time flies. I can't believe that we are about to graduate from high school and that we are going different ways in the future. I want to tell you something I have never told you. I thank God for letting us be friends. During the past four semesters, I have had such wonderful high school days with you. We went jogging together, sang together, played together, studied together, had lunch together, and chatted together. I will always remember that we counted down to the New Year together. *Those memories are so vivid that I can't forget any of them.*

Thank you for always standing by me. Sad or happy, I have had you beside me. When I confront difficulties, you are always there to comfort me, and you try to help me solve those problems. I know sometimes I lost my temper and said something bad to you, but you didn't blame me. You taught me how to control my emotions and treated me gently. If I hadn't met you, I would not know what a real friend is. *I hope that we will always be best friends no matter how far apart we are.*

Sincerely,

Amy

28. 感謝一位朋友

親愛的珊迪：

　　時間過得好快，真不敢相信我們就要高中畢業了，而且未來也將各奔東西。我想跟你說一件我從來沒告訴過你的事。我感謝上帝讓我們能當朋友。在過去的四個學期中，我跟你一起度過了愉快的高中生活。我們一起慢跑、唱歌、遊玩、唸書、吃午餐，和聊天。我會永遠記得我們一起跨年倒數。這些回憶是如此鮮明，我永遠都不會忘記。

　　謝謝你一直陪著我，不論傷心或高興，我一直有你在身旁。當我遇到困難時，你總是會出現來安慰我，你也會試著幫我解決那些問題。我知道我有的時候會發脾氣，而且會對你說一些不好聽的話，但是你都不會怪我，你會教我如何控制情緒，而且還很溫和地對待我。如果我沒遇見你，我不會知道什麼是真正的朋友。我希望不論相隔多遙遠，我們永遠都是最好的朋友。

艾咪　敬上

**

Time flies*.** 時光飛逝。　***be about to 即將
graduate〔'grædʒʊ,et〕*v.* 畢業　　past〔pæst〕*adj.* 過去的
semester〔sə'mɛstə〕*n.* 學期　　jog〔dʒɑg〕*v.* 慢跑
chat〔tʃæt〕*v.* 聊天　　***count down*** 倒數
vivid〔'vɪvɪd〕*adj.* 鮮明的；栩栩如生的　　***stand by*** 陪伴
sad or happy 無論痛苦或快樂
confront〔kən'frʌnt〕*v.* 面對　　comfort〔'kʌmfət〕*v.* 安慰
solve〔sɑlv〕*v.* 解決　　***lose one's temper*** 脾氣
blame〔blem〕*v.* 責備　　emotion〔ɪ'moʃən〕*n.* 情緒
treat〔trit〕*v.* 對待　　gently〔'dʒɛntl̩ɪ〕*adv.* 溫和地
apart〔ə'pɑrt〕*adv.* 分開地

29. A Thank-You Letter

Dear Jeremy Kang,

I am writing to you on behalf of the group from Jianguo High School that visited your department last week. *We all had a wonderful time and found the tour very informative.* We learned a lot about the field of physics and the course of study and National Tsing Hua University. This knowledge will help every one of us to make important decisions about our futures. As for me, I was so impressed with what I saw that I am now certain that I would like to study at your university if I have the chance.

Most important of all, I would like to express my appreciation to you personally for everything you did. You made us feel very welcome and answered all of our questions patiently. *Of course,* we will share our great experience with other students. I hope that another group from our high school will be able to visit you in the future.

Sincerely,
Mark Lin

29.　一封感謝函

親愛的康傑洛米：

　　我謹代表上星期前往貴系的建國中學參訪團，寫這封信給您。我們都感到很愉快，並且覺得這次行程使我們獲益良多。我們知道很多關於物理學這個領域的事，以及學習的過程，也更了解國立清華大學。這些知識將會幫助我們每個人，做出跟我們的未來有關的重要決定。至於我，我對所看到的一切印象很深刻，所以現在非常確定，如果有機會，我想要就讀清華大學。

　　最重要的是，對於您所做的一切，我個人想要表達我的感激之意。您使我們覺得很受歡迎，並且很有耐心地回答我們所有的問題。當然，我們會把這麼棒的經驗和其他的同學分享。我希望敝高中的另一個參訪團未來也能去拜訪你們。

　　　　　　　　　　　　　　　　　林馬克　敬上

** ────────────────────────

on behalf of 代表　　department (dɪˈpɑrtmənt) *n.* 系
have a wonderful time 玩得愉快　　find (faɪnd) *v.* 覺得
tour (tʊr) *n.* (考察、巡視等) 短期旅行
informative (ɪnˈfɔrmətɪv) *adj.* 提供知識的；有教育性的
field (fild) *n.* 領域　　physics (ˈfɪzɪks) *n.* 物理學
course (kors) *n.* 過程　　***make a decision*** 做決定
as for 至於　　***be impressed with*** 對…印象深刻
most important of all 最重要的是　　***would like*** 想要
express (ɪkˈsprɛs) *v.* 表達
appreciation (ə،prɪʃɪˈeʃən) *n.* 感激
personally (ˈpɝsṇlɪ) *adv.* 親自
welcome (ˈwɛlkəm) *adj.* 受歡迎的
patiently (ˈpeʃəntlɪ) *adv.* 有耐心地　　share (ʃɛr) *v.* 分享

30. A Letter to a Teacher

Dear Ms. Lin,

Long time no see! I have been enjoying college life. *However*, I often think of you and the help you gave me in high school. I suppose that without your encouragement, I wouldn't be here today. *So I would like to express my appreciation for all your support*.

College life has been challenging. But as I learned from you, knowledge is power. Learning is the most interesting thing in the world. Thanks to your inspiration, my mind is now a sponge for knowledge. I'll never forget how I used to be late with my homework. Unlike other teachers, you never scolded me. *Instead*, you said, "Never put off until tomorrow what you can do today." This has become my motto in college. Now I am striving to achieve great things.

In closing, I would like to mention one thing. That is, as a result of your example, I plan to become a high school teacher, too! It would be an honor to follow in your footsteps. *I hope I can be as inspirational to my students as you were to me*. Thank you again.

Best wishes,

Helen

30. 給老師的一封信

親愛的林老師：

　　好久不見！我很喜歡大學生活，但是，我還是常想到您，還有高中時您給我的幫助。我想，沒有您的鼓勵，就沒有今天的我，所以我想要感謝您對我的支持。

　　大學生活很有挑戰性，但是就像我跟您學到的，知識就是力量，學習是全世界最有趣的事情。因為您的激勵，現在我的腦海中就像一塊海綿，不斷吸收知識。我不會忘記之前我常遲交功課，您不像其他老師，從來沒罵過我，您反而會說：「今日事，今日畢。」這成了我唸大學時的座右銘，現在我很努力要做很多大事。

　　在這封信的最後，我還想說一件事，那就是，因為有您做榜樣，我也打算要成為一名高中老師！能追隨您的腳步是我的光榮。我希望可以激勵我的學生，就像您之前激勵我一樣。我要再次感謝您。

　　　　　　　　　　　　　寄上由衷的祝福，
　　　　　　　　　　　　　　海倫

** ————————————————

suppose〔sə'poz〕v. 認為
encouragement〔ɪn'kɝɪdʒmənt〕n. 鼓勵
appreciation〔ə͵priʃɪ'eʃən〕n. 感激
challenging〔'tʃælɪndʒɪŋ〕adj. 具有挑戰性的　　***thanks to*** 由於
inspiration〔͵ɪnspə'reʃən〕n. 激勵　　　sponge〔spʌndʒ〕n. 海綿
used to 以前　　　scold〔skold〕v. 責罵
instead〔ɪn'stɛd〕adv. 取而代之；反而　　***put off*** 拖延
motto〔'mɑto〕n. 座右銘　　　strive〔straɪv〕v. 努力
achieve〔ə'tʃiv〕n. 達成　　　***in closing*** 總之
as a result of 由於　　　example〔ɪg'zæmpļ〕n. 榜樣；模範
follow in one's ***footsteps*** 追隨…的腳步
inspirational〔͵ɪnspə'reʃənļ〕adj. 鼓舞人心的

31. **Happy Birthday!**

Dear Dad,

Today is your fiftieth birthday. I'd like to say happy birthday to you first. Since I was born, you have been taking care of me. It has been almost eighteen years since then. Although you have so much work to do, so many meetings to attend, and so many lectures to deliver, you always look after me. *I am very thankful that you make me such a priority and that I have such an important place in your heart.*

You are my idol. You always do things properly and efficiently, and that is why I admire you. *However,* please don't work too hard. Take good care of yourself, too. *Nothing is worth more than health. In the future,* I hope that I can be a man like you.

Happy Birthday!

Sincerely,

Alex

31. 生日快樂！

親愛的老爸：

　　今天是您五十歲生日，首先我想跟您說聲生日快樂。自從我出生以來，您就一直照顧我，從那時起到現在已經快十八年了，雖然您有這麼多的工作要做，有這麼多的會議要參加，有這麼多的演說要發表，您都一直照顧我。我很感激您這麼重視我，我在您的心中能有這麼重要的地位。

　　您是我的偶像。您做事總是妥當又有效率，這也是我這麼欽佩您的原因。但是，工作請別太辛勞，要好好照顧自己。健康是最珍貴的。未來，我希望自己也能成為跟您一樣的人。

　　生日快樂！

　　　　　　　　　　　　　　　愛力克斯　敬上

＊＊ —————————————————————

take care of 照顧　　***since then*** 從那時起

meeting〔'mitɪŋ〕*n.* 會議　　attend〔ə'tɛnd〕*v.* 參加

lecture〔'lɛktʃə〕*n.* 演講　　deliver〔dɪ'lɪvə〕*v.* 發表

look after 照顧　　thankful〔'θæŋkfəl〕*adj.* 感激的

priority〔praɪ'ɔrətɪ〕*n.* 優先

heart〔hɑrt〕*n.* 心　　idol〔'aɪdḷ〕*n.* 偶像

properly〔'prɑpəlɪ〕*adv.* 適當地

efficiently〔ə'fɪʃəntlɪ〕*adv.* 有效率地

admire〔əd'maɪr〕*v.* 欽佩

32. Thanking a Teacher

Dear Ms. Lee,

You probably remember me as a naïve little elementary school student. It might surprise you to know that I have become a mature high school student. I owe it all to you. I benefited so much from your painstaking teaching and wonderful philosophy of life. You embraced every student's disadvantages and set us all on the right track when we made a mistake. I still miss your kind words and thoughtful advice. *You have had such a great influence on my life that I will always consider you my best guide.*

Now I am doing well in high school. I'm getting good grades, but what is more important is that I get along well with all of my classmates. Thanks to your example, I am more considerate of others. *When I find that someone is suffering from a difficulty, I do my best to give him a hand. Well goes the saying,* "It is better to give than to receive." Now I understand why you helped without any complaints and I know that practicing benevolence is the best thing I can do in my life. *To sum up,* thank you for your wonderful teaching.

Best wishes,
Eddie Chen

32. 感謝老師

親愛的李老師：

　　在您的印象中，我可能還只是個天眞的小學生吧。知道我已是一個成熟的高中生，您可能會很驚訝，這一切都要歸功於您。我從您盡心的教導以及很棒的人生觀中獲益良多。您接受每個學生的缺點，並在我們犯錯的時候將我們導回正軌。我還是很想念您的金玉良言以及苦口婆心的勸導。您對我的人生影響深遠，我永遠會將您當作是我最棒的導師。

　　現在我在高中表現得不錯，我的成績很好，但是更重要的是，我跟同學都能和睦相處。因爲您樹立的榜樣，我現在比較能體貼別人。當我發現同學有困難，我都會盡力幫助他。俗話說得好：「施比受更有福。」現在我才能體會爲什麼您要無怨無尤地幫助別人，我也知道做善事是人生中最棒的事。總之，感謝您這麼棒的教誨。

寄上衷心的祝福，

陳艾迪

** ─────

naïve〔nɑˋiv〕*adj.* 天眞的　　mature〔məˋtʊr〕*adj.* 成熟的

owe sth. to sb. 將某事歸功於某人　　benefit〔ˋbɛnəfɪt〕*v.* 獲益

painstaking〔ˋpenzͺtekɪŋ〕*adj.* 不辭勞苦的；盡心的

philosophy of life 人生觀　　embrace〔ɪmˋbres〕*v.* 欣然接受

disadvantage〔ͺdɪsədˋvæntɪdʒ〕*n.* 缺點

set〔sɛt〕*v.* 使…成爲（某種狀態）　　track〔træk〕*n.* 軌道

thoughtful〔ˋθɔtfəl〕*adj.* 體貼的　　guide〔gaɪd〕*n.* 引導者

do well 表現好　　***get along well with*** 與…和睦相處

suffer from 受…之苦　　***give sb. a hand*** 幫助某人

well goes the saying 俗話說得好

complaint〔kəmˋplent〕*n.* 抱怨

practice〔ˋpræktɪs〕*v.* 執行；做；從事

benevolence〔bəˋnɛvələns〕*n.* 善行　　***to sum up*** 總之

33. A Letter of Apology

Dear Jack,

I am so sorry for making you wait yesterday. Please believe that I would never do that to you on purpose. As I explained yesterday, I overslept and, and by the time I woke up, I was already an hour late. I raced to the department store as fast as I could, but it still took me another hour to arrive. Imagine my surprise to find you still waiting there. You were not even angry; you were just worried that something bad had happened to me. *What a true friend you are!*

I really want to make it up to you, so please allow me to treat you to something that you like. How about lunch or a trip to the movies? *Most important of all,* I promise that I will never make this mistake again. The next time we have plans to do something together, I will be sure to arrive early and wait for you!

Sincerely,

Sam

33. 道　歉　信

親愛的傑克：

　　很抱歉昨天讓你等我，請你相信我絕不是故意那樣
對你。就像我昨天解釋的，我睡過頭了，當我起床的時
候，我已經遲到一個小時。我儘快衝去百貨公司，不過
這又花了我一個小時的時間。想像一下，當我發現你還
在那裡等我的時候，我有多驚訝。你甚至沒有生氣；你
只是擔心我是不是出事了。你真的是我真正的朋友！

　　我真的很想補償你，所以請讓我請你一些你喜歡的
東西。你覺得一頓午餐或一場電影怎麼樣？最重要的
是，我保證絕不會再犯這樣的錯誤。下次我們打算一起
出去的時候，我一定會提早去等你！

　　　　　　　　　　　　　　　　　　　山姆　敬上

**

apology〔ə'pɑlədʒɪ〕*n.* 道歉
on purpose 故意地
oversleep〔'ovɚ'slip〕*v.* 睡過頭
by the time 到…的時候　　*wake up* 醒來
race〔res〕*v.*（快）跑
make up 補償　　treat〔trit〕*v.* 招待
a trip to the movies 去看電影
promise〔'prɑmɪs〕*v.* 保證
imagine〔ɪ'mædʒɪn〕*v.* 想像
sincerely〔sɪn'sɪrlɪ〕*adv.* 真誠地；誠摯地

34. An Apology to a Teacher

Dear Ms. Lin,

I would like to apologize for my behavior in class yesterday. I know it was wrong for me to use my cell phone in class, especially after you asked me to stop. It was very disrespectful and disruptive.

I know it is no excuse, but I received the cell phone yesterday as a gift. I was so excited about it that I simply could not resist the temptation to play with it. *I truly regret what I did, and I hope that you can forgive me. I promise that it will never happen again.*

Not only will I pay full attention in your class, but I will also turn off my phone before I enter the room. I say this not just because I want your forgiveness. I am sincerely sorry about and embarrassed by my behavior. I really do value your teaching. I hope you will give me another chance.

Sincerely yours,

Sam

34.　向老師道歉

親愛的林老師：

　　我想要爲我昨天在課堂上的行爲道歉。我知道上課時使用手機是我的錯，尤其是在您制止我之後。這眞的是非常不禮貌，而且也會擾亂上課秩序。

　　我知道這不是藉口，不過我是昨天才收到這支別人送我的手機。我很興奮，無法抗拒要玩這支手機的誘惑。我眞的很後悔自己的所作所爲，我希望您能原諒我。我保證絕不再犯。

　　我不僅上您的課時會全神貫注，而且也會在進入教室之前先把手機關掉。我這麼說不只是因爲想獲得您的原諒，我眞心地爲我的行爲感到抱歉，也覺得尷尬。我眞的很重視您的教學。我希望您能再給我一次機會。

山姆　敬上

** ————————————————————

apologize〔ə'pɑlə,dʒaɪz〕v. 道歉　　*cell phone* 手機
disrespectful〔,dɪsrɪ'spɛktfəl〕adj. 失禮的
disruptive〔dɪs'rʌptɪv〕adj. 破壞性的；擾亂的
excuse〔ɪk'skjus〕n. 藉口
resist〔rɪ'zɪst〕v. 抵抗；抗拒
temptation〔tɛmp'teʃən〕n. 誘惑
regret〔rɪ'grɛt〕v. 後悔　　*not only...but also* 不僅…而且
pay full attention 全神貫注　　*turn off* 關掉
forgiveness〔fə'gɪvnɪs〕n. 原諒
sincerely〔sɪn'sɪrlɪ〕adv. 由衷地；眞誠地
embarrassed〔ɪm'bærəst〕adj. 感到尷尬的
value〔'vælju〕v. 重視　　teaching〔'titʃɪŋ〕n. 教學

35. Breaking Bad News to My Mother

Dear Mother,

I have some bad news to share. Last week, I lost the new smart phone you gave me. It happened at school. Before I went to play basketball, I placed the phone on a bench near the court. It was right next to my jacket and gym bag. After the game, I left, taking my jacket and bag. *But* I forgot the phone. It wasn't until 10 minutes later that I noticed. I quickly ran back to school, but the phone was nowhere to be found.

I am very sorry that I lost the phone. I know you intended for me to make good use of it. *Plus*, smart phones are much more expensive than regular cell phones. *It was clearly irresponsible of me to lose it.* *However*, I have figured out how to prevent it from happening again.

From now on, I will not bring important items when I play sports. If I have to, I will ask a friend to hold them for me. This includes my cell phone and other expensive things. *In the end*, I have learned a lesson. *That is*, to be careful with my possessions.

Sincerely,

Carl

35. 向媽媽透露壞消息

親愛的媽媽：

　　我有壞消息要告訴妳。上禮拜，我弄丟了妳給我的智慧型手機，是在學校弄丟的。在我去打籃球之前，我把它放在球場附近的長椅上，就在我的夾克和健身袋的旁邊。比賽結束後，我拿了夾克和袋子就離開了，不過我忘了手機，直到十分鐘之後我才注意到。我很快地跑回學校，但是到處都找不到我的手機。

　　我很抱歉我遺失手機。我知道妳想要我好好利用這支手機，而且智慧型手機比一般的手機貴很多。遺失手機顯然是我太不負責任了。不過，我已經想好要如何預防這種情況再度發生。

　　從現在開始，當我從事體育運動時，我不會帶重要的物品。如果必須帶，我會請朋友替我拿著，這包括我的手機和其他貴重的東西。最後，我已經學到教訓，那就是要小心保管自己的物品。

卡爾　敬上

**

break〔brek〕*v.* 透露；說出　　share〔ʃɛr〕*v.* 分享
smart phone 智慧型手機　　place〔ples〕*v.* 放置
bench〔bɛntʃ〕*n.* 長椅　　court〔kort〕*n.* (網球、籃球等) 球場
gym〔dʒɪm〕*n.* 健身房 (= *gymnasium*)　　*gym bag* 健身袋
notice〔'notɪs〕*v.* 注意到　　intend〔ɪn'tɛnd〕*v.* 打算
plus〔plʌs〕*adv.* 而且；此外　　regular〔'rɛgjələ〕*adj.* 普通的
cell phone 手機　　*from now on* 從現在起
item〔'aɪtəm〕*n.* 項目；物品　　*play sports* 從事體育運動
hold〔hold〕*v.* 拿著　　*in the end* 最後
learn a lesson 學到教訓
possessions〔pə'zɛʃənz〕*n. pl.* 所有物

36. Begging Forgiveness of a Friend

Dear George,

I'm really sorry about what I did to you. I shouldn't have laughed at you when you were upset. I was heartless and insensitive when you got a poor grade. I know that it really annoyed you. I didn't mean it. I know I was a lousy friend. But please listen to my reason.

I just wanted to inspire you to try harder. I wanted to change your lazy attitude. I'm really sorry. I know what I did wasn't justified. Now, I just beg for your mercy. I hope you can forgive me. I promise I won't do it again.

And now, I know what we should do: I will study with you and we can improve together. Maybe when we have questions, we can help each other. *When one of us wants to give up, the other can be a pillar of support.* Please forgive me. Let's be friends again!

Best wishes,

Helen

36. 請求朋友原諒

親愛的喬治：

我對我的所作所爲眞的很抱歉，我不該在你沮喪的時候嘲笑你。我在你成績不好的時候這樣做，眞的是太無情、太不體貼了。我知道這會讓你很生氣，但我不是故意的。我知道我是一個差勁的朋友，但請聽聽我的理由。

我只是想要激勵你再努力一點，我想改變你懶惰的態度。我眞的很抱歉，我知道這樣做很沒有道理。現在我只想要你的諒解，我希望你能原諒我，我保證絕不再犯。

現在，我知道我們該怎麼做：我會跟你一起唸書，我們可以一起進步，或許當我們有問題時，可以互相幫忙。當我們其中有一個人要放棄時，另一個可以當精神支柱。請原諒我。讓我們重新當朋友吧！

> 寄上由衷的祝福，
> 海倫

** ─────────────────

beg *sth. of sb.* 向某人請求某物
forgiveness〔fə'ɡɪvnɪs〕*n.* 原諒   ***laugh at*** 嘲笑
upset〔ʌp'sɛt〕*adj.* 沮喪的；不高興的
heartless〔'hɑrtlɪs〕*adj.* 無情的
insensitive〔ɪn'sɛnsətɪv〕*adj.* 不體貼的；不敏感的
annoy〔ə'nɔɪ〕*v.* 使生氣   ***I didn't mean it.*** 我不是有意的。
lousy〔'laʊzɪ〕*adj.* 糟糕的   inspire〔ɪn'spaɪr〕*v.* 鼓勵
try harder 更努力   justified〔'dʒʌstə,faɪd〕*adj.* 應該的；正當的
mercy〔'mɝsɪ〕*n.* 慈悲   improve〔ɪm'pruv〕*v.* 改善；進步
give up 放棄   pillar〔'pɪlə〕*n.*（精神）支柱
forgive〔fə'ɡɪv〕*v.* 原諒

37. An Apology for Speaking Out of Turn

Dear Ms. Lin,

Please forgive my behavior in class the other day. I was out of line. A student should never think he knows more than the teacher. A student should listen to the lesson. If he has questions, he can ask. *Otherwise,* right or wrong, it is not his place to correct the teacher.

Allow me to explain my actions. Of course, this does not excuse my behavior. *I just want you to know where I was coming from.* I consider myself somewhat of an amateur archaeologist. Since we were discussing ancient history, I felt justified in expressing my opinions. *However,* it was impolite of me to interrupt. I did not take your feelings into consideration. For that I deeply apologize.

You are one of the best teachers in the school. I have always held you in high esteem. I hope you will not let my one rude outburst affect our student-teacher relationship. *From now on,* I will choose my words carefully and think before I speak. *I hope you understand my sincerity and find it in your heart to forgive me.*

Your student,

Sam

37. 一封爲出言不遜而道歉的信

親愛的林老師：

　　請原諒我前幾天在課堂上的行爲。我太過份了，學生絕不該認爲自己知道的比老師多，應該要認眞聽課。如果有問題，可以發問，否則，不論對錯，都不該糾正老師。

　　讓我解釋一下我的行爲。當然，我不是要替自己的行爲找藉口。我只是要讓您知道我的想法。我認爲自己是個業餘的考古學家，旣然我們在討論古代歷史，所以我覺得表達我的看法是很合理的。但是我插嘴是很不禮貌的，我沒考慮到您的感受，對於這一點，我深感抱歉。

　　您是學校最好的老師之一，我一直很敬重您。我希望這次不禮貌的情緒失控，不會影響我們的師生關係，從現在起，我說話會小心，而且說話前會先經大腦思考。希望您能了解我的誠意，並且能儘量原諒我。

您的學生，

山姆

** ───────────────────

out of turn 輕率地　　forgive〔fɚ'gɪv〕v. 原諒

the other day 前幾天　　***out of line*** 過份

right or wrong 不論對錯　　excuse〔ɪk'skjuz〕v. 替…找藉口

where I was coming from 我當時的想法（ = *my side of the story* ）；

　　我當時爲什麼會那樣（ = *why I acted the way I did* ）

somewhat〔'sʌm,hwɑt〕adv. 稍微；有點

amateur〔'æmə,tʃur〕adj. 業餘的

archaeologist〔,ɑrkɪ'ɑlədʒɪst〕n. 考古學家

ancient〔'enʃənt〕adj. 古代的　　justified〔'dʒʌstə,faɪd〕adj. 合理的

interrupt〔,ɪntə'rʌpt〕v. 打斷　　***take ~ into consideration*** 考慮到~

hold sb. in high esteem 敬重某人

outburst〔'aut,bɝst〕n.（情感）爆發　　affect〔ə'fɛkt〕v. 影響

find it in one's heart（心中雖然不願意）儘量

38. Cancellation Due to a Personal Matter

Dear Ken,

First, I want to say sorry. I can't go on the class trip you planned for us. I know it is tomorrow and I have already paid the fee. Don't worry about the money. I don't expect a refund. Please accept my apology for backing out at the last minute. *However*, my reason for cancelling is very serious.

Actually, my grandfather, who is 89 years old, is very ill. He has a serious heart condition. He may only have few days to live. All of my family members will be at the hospital to see him. *We must be there for him in his time of need*. It might be the last chance to see him alive. Surely you understand. *Family comes before everything else*.

I hope the trip is a success and you have fun. I'm sad that I will miss the experience. *However*, I ask that you will add my grandfather to your prayers.

Best wishes,
Jack

38. 因故無法參加班遊

親愛的肯：

　　首先，我想先說抱歉，我無法參加你替我們規劃的班遊。我知道日期是明天，而且我也已經繳交費用了。不過別擔心錢，我不用退費。請接受我最後一刻才要退出的道歉，但是我取消的原因是非常嚴重的。

　　其實，我八十九歲的爺爺病得很重。我爺爺心臟的狀況很不好，他可能只剩幾天的生命。所有的家人都會到醫院看他。我們一定得在他需要我們的時候陪他。這可能是最後一面了，你一定能了解，因為家人比什麼都重要。

　　我希望班遊能成功，你們也能玩得高興。錯過這次班遊我會很難過。但我希望你在禱告的時候，也能幫我爺爺禱告。

寄上由衷的祝福，
傑克

**　**

cancellation〔ˌkænsḷˈeʃən〕 n. 取消　　matter〔ˈmætɚ〕 n. 事情
fee〔fi〕 n. 費用　　expect〔ɪkˈspɛkt〕 v. 期待
refund〔ˈriˌfʌnd〕 n. 退錢　　accept〔əkˈsɛpt〕 v. 接受
apology〔əˈpɑlədʒɪ〕 n. 道歉　　***back out*** 退出
at the last minute 在最後一刻　　cancel〔ˈkænsḷ〕 v. 取消
serious〔ˈsɪrɪəs〕 adj. 認真的；嚴肅的；嚴重的
ill〔ɪl〕 adj. 生病的
condition〔kənˈdɪʃən〕 n.（身體）異常
alive〔əˈlaɪv〕 adj. 活的　　***come before*** 位於…之前；比…重要
success〔səkˈsɛs〕 n. 成功的事情　　***have fun*** 玩得愉快
experience〔ɪkˈspɪrɪəns〕 n. 經驗；體驗
add A to B 把 A 加到 B　　prayer〔prɛr〕 n. 祈禱

39. Asking for a Rain Check

Dear Sally,

I am sorry that I have to write this letter to you. I know we planned to go to the exhibition next weekend. I was really looking forward to it. *However*, I forgot that I had a previous engagement. I was invited to play the piano for a charity event.

You know that I devote myself to charity work and it means a lot to me. *So I have no choice but to reschedule our date.* I know it is not like me to break a date and I am really sorry for that. *Thus*, I'm asking for a rain check. To make it up to you, I want to invite you to go to the exhibition on the following weekend, and this time I will pay for the tickets.

I know this cancellation will spoil our original plans, but I really want to go to the exhibition with you. *I hope you accept my apology and are willing to compromise.*

Sincerely,
Debbie

39. 要求改期

親愛的莎莉：

寫這封信給妳我很抱歉。我知道我們計畫下個週末要去看展覽，我很期待能跟妳一起去，但是我忘記我之前跟人家有約，我受邀為一場慈善活動演奏鋼琴。

你知道我本身很投入慈善活動，它對我來說意義重大。所以我不得不重新安排跟你去看展覽的日期。我知道我不像是會爽約的人，我真的感到很抱歉。所以我想跟妳改個日期。為了彌補妳，我想邀妳下週末去看展覽，而且我會付門票。

我知道取消這次約會，會破壞我們原先的計畫，但是我真的想跟妳一起去看展覽。希望妳能接受我的道歉，願意妥協一下。

黛比　敬上

**

rain check 改期；雨天延期入場憑證

exhibition〔͵ɛksə'bɪʃən〕*n.* 展覽　　*look forward to* 期待

previous〔'privɪəs〕*adj.* 先前的

engagement〔ɪn'gedʒmənt〕*n.* 約定

charity〔'tʃærətɪ〕*n.* 慈善　　event〔ɪ'vɛnt〕*n.* 大型活動

devote〔dɪ'vot〕*v.* 奉獻；使致力於

devote oneself to 致力於

have no choice but to V. 不得不…

reschedule〔ri'skɛdʒul〕*v.* 重新安排時間

break〔brek〕*v.* 違背；未遵守　　*make it up to sb.* 補償某人

following〔'faloɪŋ〕*adj.* 接下來的

cancellation〔͵kænsḷ'eʃən〕*n.* 取消　　spoil〔spɔɪl〕*v.* 破壞

original〔ə'rɪdʒənḷ〕*adj.* 原本的

apology〔ə'palədʒɪ〕*n.* 道歉　　*be willing to* 願意

compromise〔'kamprə͵maɪz〕*v.* 妥協

40. An Apology for Behaving Inappropriately

Dear Robert,

I have given it a lot of thought. Even though you may not want to hear what I have to say, please listen. I wish to offer my sincere apology. I definitely went too far in my attempt to pull a practical joke.

Believe me, I did not mean for it to happen that way. I honestly did not think the stunt would ruin your shoes. You have no idea how bad I felt. *To make it up to you, I was determined to right my wrong.* I went to the mall to buy you a new pair of shoes. But they were sold out! You have no idea how upset I was!

Now you aren't speaking to me. I believe that I deserve your scorn. Now the only thing I can do is beg your forgiveness. I hope this letter shows that I want to be a good friend. I am willing to do anything to save our friendship. *Please forgive me and give me a second chance.*

Sincerely,

James

40. 爲行爲不當道歉

親愛的羅伯特：

　　我想很久了，雖然你可能不想聽我要說的話，但是還是希望你能聽。我眞心地跟你道歉，我的惡作劇實在是太過份了。

　　相信我，我不是故意要這樣的，我眞的不知道這個愚蠢的行爲會弄壞你的鞋子。你不知道那時我有多難受。爲了補償你，我決定要彌補我的錯，我跑去購物中心，想買一雙新鞋給你。但是你的鞋子竟然賣光了！你不知道我有多沮喪！

　　現在你都不跟我說話，我想你看不起我是應該的。現在我唯一能做的，就是請求你的原諒。我希望這封信能讓你知道，我想要當一個好朋友。我願意做任何事情來挽救我們的友誼。請原諒我，再給我一次機會。

　　　　　　　　　　　　　　　　　　　　詹姆士　敬上

** ——————————————————————

apology〔ə'pɑlədʒɪ〕*n.* 道歉　　behave〔bɪ'hev〕*v.* 行爲
inappropriately〔ˌɪnə'proprɪɪtlɪ〕*adv.* 不適當地
thought〔θɔt〕*n.* 思考；想法　　offer〔'ɔfɚ〕*v.* 提供
sincere〔sɪn'sɪr〕*adj.* 誠摯的
definitely〔'dɛfənɪtlɪ〕*adv.* 確實地　　***go too far*** 太過份
attempt〔ə'tɛmpt〕*n.* 嘗試　　pull〔pʊl〕*v.* 實行；做
practical joke 惡作劇（= *prank*）
honestly〔'ɑnɪstlɪ〕*adv.* 誠實地；實在
stunt〔stʌnt〕*n.* 愚蠢的行爲　　ruin〔'ruɪn〕*v.* 破壞
make it up to sb. 補償某人；彌補某人
determined〔dɪ'tɜmɪnd〕*adj.* 下定決心的　　right〔raɪt〕*v.* 改正
wrong〔rɔŋ〕*n.* 錯誤　　mall〔mɔl〕*n.* 購物中心
be sold out 賣光　　upset〔ʌp'sɛt〕*adj.* 難過的；生氣的
deserve〔dɪ'zɜv〕*v.* 值得；應得　　scorn〔skɔrn〕*n.* 輕視
beg〔bɛg〕*v.* 請求　　forgiveness〔fɚ'gɪvnɪs〕*n.* 原諒
save〔sev〕*v.* 挽救　　second〔'sɛkənd〕*adj.* 另外的

41. An Apology for Telling a Lie

Dear Ken,

Maybe you have forgotten the glass miniature of your favorite cartoon character, which you gave me as a present several years ago; *however*, I still remember it vividly. *That day*, I showed appreciation for it and asked if you would lend it to me for a few days. Without hesitation, you put it in my hands carefully even though you really adored it.

Unfortunately, I was so careless that I dropped it and it shattered into pieces. *I couldn't summon up the courage to tell you I had broken it for fear that our friendship would vanish. Therefore*, I just asked you to give it to me as my birthday gift instead of telling you the cruel truth.

Since then, I have regretted it. I hope you can forgive me. *Moreover*, maybe we can go to buy the same miniature. I would like to do that for you to show you how much I value our priceless friendship.

Sincerely,

Jack

41. 因為說謊而道歉

親愛的肯恩：

　　也許你已經忘了那個你最喜歡的玻璃卡通人物公仔，那是你好幾年前送給我的禮物；不過我仍然記得很清楚。那天，我很欣賞那個公仔，所以就問你，可不可以借我玩幾天。你毫不猶豫，小心地把它放在我的手中，即使你真的很喜歡它。

　　遺憾的是，我很不小心，把它摔成碎片。我無法鼓起勇氣告訴你，我把它打破了，唯恐我們的友情會消失。因此，我只是請你把它當作生日禮物送給我，而不告訴你這個殘酷的真相。

　　從那時起，我就一直很後悔。我希望你能原諒我。此外，或許我們可以一起去買一樣的公仔。我想為你這麼做，以表示我有多麼重視我們寶貴的友誼。

傑克　敬上

** ————————————————————

miniature〔'mɪnɪətʃɚ〕*n.* 微小的模型；公仔
character〔'kærɪktɚ〕*n.* 人物　　present〔'prɛznt〕*n.* 禮物
vividly〔'vɪvɪdlɪ〕*adj.* 生動地
appreciation〔ə,priʃɪ'eʃən〕*n.* 欣賞
hesitation〔,hɛzə'teʃən〕*n.* 猶豫　　*even though* 即使
adore〔ə'dor〕*v.* 極喜愛
unfortunately〔ʌn'fɔrtʃənɪtlɪ〕*adv.* 不幸地；遺憾地
shatter〔'ʃætɚ〕*v.* 變成粉粹　　summon〔'sʌmən〕*v.* 鼓起（勇氣）
summon up courage 鼓起勇氣　　*for fear that* 以免；惟恐
vanish〔'vænɪʃ〕*v.* 消失　　*birthday gift* 生日禮物
cruel〔'kruəl〕*adj.* 殘忍的　　regret〔rɪ'grɛt〕*v.* 後悔
priceless〔'praɪslɪs〕*adj.* 無價的

42. Apology for an Academic Failure

Dear Teacher,

I can't believe I failed the English mid-term exam. Even though my grades are not great, I thought I would do better. This is a nightmare. I stayed up late every night this week. I studied as hard as I could. But to receive a failing grade is beyond my imagination. If I had known I would fail so miserably, I wouldn't have studied so hard.

I am so sorry for my performance. I let myself down. *Worst of all*, I feel like I let you down. You have been so patient with me. *However*, I am more determined than ever to succeed. I have decided to use a reference book to improve my English skills. *In addition*, I will practice my listening skills with a CD. *Meanwhile*, I will limit my study time each day. I feel that perhaps I studied too much, and therefore, I didn't retain any information in my memory.

This failure has been hard to accept. *But I will double my efforts and try harder*. Please forgive me this time. It won't happen again.

Your student,
Charles

42. 因為成績不好而道歉

親愛的老師：

　　我真不敢相信，我英文期中考不及格。即使我的成績並不好，但我還以為我會考得更好。這真是個惡夢。這星期我每天晚上都熬夜到很晚，我儘可能用功讀書，但是考不及格實在是超乎我的想像。如果我知道會考這麼糟，我就不會這麼用功了。

　　對於我的表現，我覺得很抱歉，我讓自己失望了，最糟的是，我覺得我好像也讓您失望了。您一直對我很有耐心。不過，我現在比以前更堅決要成功。我已經決定，要用參考書來增進我的英文能力。此外，我會用 CD 來練習我的聽力。同時，我會限制自己每天的讀書時間。我覺得也許是因為我讀書時間太長，所以才記不住任何內容。

　　這次的失敗令人難以接受。不過我會加倍努力，並且更用功。請原諒我這一次。這種情形絕不會再發生。

　　　　　　　　　　　　　　　　　　您的學生，
　　　　　　　　　　　　　　　　　　查爾斯

**

academic〔͵ækə'dɛmɪk〕*adj.* 學術的　　fail〔fel〕*v.* 考不及格
mid-term exam 期中考　　grade〔gred〕*n.* 成績
nightmare〔'naɪt͵mɛr〕*n.* 惡夢　　*stay up* 熬夜
as...as one can 儘可能（ *= as...as possible* ）
beyond one's imagination 超出某人的想像
miserably〔'mɪzərəblɪ〕*adv.* 悲慘地
performance〔pə'fɔrməns〕*n.* 表現
let sb. down 讓某人失望　　*worst of all* 最糟的是
patient〔'peʃənt〕*adj.* 有耐心的
determined〔dɪ'tɜmɪnd〕*adj.* 堅決的　　*than ever* 比以前
reference book 參考書　　meanwhile〔'mɪn͵hwaɪl〕*adv.* 同時
retain〔rɪ'ten〕*v.* 保留　　double〔'dʌbl̩〕*v.* 使加倍

43. Let's Stay in Touch!

Dear Lisa,

　　Time goes fast. We will graduate soon. We have been friends for three years. I can't believe that we have to say goodbye. *Well,* that's the point of the letter. I don't want to say goodbye. I'd much rather say "See you later."

　　I remember that when I was in grade one, I was so shy. I was afraid to talk to others. Everyone made jokes and played with each other, but I was lonely. I sat at my desk quietly. You were the first one to talk to me. You introduced me to your friends.

　　After some time, I became like a member of your family. You treated me like a sister. When I was upset, you always cheered me up. You helped me solve my problems. How lucky I am to have a friend like you! *Your warm smile wipes away my troubles.* Your care gives me the power to carry on. Now, we are going to go to college. I just want to say one thing. *Whatever happens, let's never lose touch with each other.*

　　　　　　　　　　　　　　　　Yours truly,

　　　　　　　　　　　　　　　　Tina

43. 保持聯絡！

親愛的麗莎：

　　時間過得眞快，不久我們就要畢業了。我們當了三年的朋友，眞不敢相信我們就要說再見了。嗯，雖然那是這封信的目的，但是我不想說再見，我倒寧願說：「待會兒見。」

　　記得我唸一年級的時候，我很害羞，很怕跟別人說話。每個人都有說有笑地玩在一起，但是我很孤單，我安靜地坐在座位上。你是第一個跟我說話的人，你還介紹你的朋友給我認識。

　　過了一段時間之後，我變成就像你的家人一般，你把我當成姊妹來看待。我傷心的時候，你總是會逗我開心。你幫助我解決問題，我好幸運能有像你這樣的朋友！你溫暖的微笑掃去我的煩惱，你的關心讓我有堅持下去的力量。現在，我們就要上大學了，我只想對你說一句話，無論發生什麼事，我們絕對不能失去聯絡。

蒂娜　敬上

＊＊

Time goes fast. 時光飛逝 (= *Time flies.*)

point〔 pɔɪnt 〕*n.* 目的　　graduate〔'grædʒʊˌet 〕*v.* 畢業

would rather 寧願　　grade〔 gred 〕*n.* 年級

shy〔 ʃaɪ 〕*adj.* 害羞的　　***make a joke*** 說笑話

introduce〔ˌɪntrə'djus 〕*v.* 介紹

treat〔 trit 〕*v.* 對待　　upset〔 ʌp'sɛt 〕*adj.* 不高興的

cheer sb. up 逗某人開心；激勵某人　　***wipe away*** 掃除

trouble〔'trʌbḷ 〕*n.* 困難；煩惱　　care〔 kɛr 〕*n.* 關心

carry on 繼續　　***lose touch*** 失去聯絡

44. Getting Back in Touch

Dear Kevin,

It has been three years since we graduated from junior high school and you emigrated. I was so happy to get back in touch with you. We certainly have a lot to catch up on. You asked about my high school life and club activities, so let me tell you a little about them.

Of course, you remember what junior high was like. *The biggest difference in high school is that we have more freedom. We also have more responsibility.* Our teachers don't tell us exactly what to study and when, but we still have to study hard! There is a lot of pressure to get good grades. As for the clubs, there are a lot of good choices. That means that we can find a club that we are really keen to join. *Besides*, the clubs are much more interesting, and you can even give a performance on formal occasions if you practice hard. I joined the guitar club this year, and I love it!

There are still a lot of things I would like to tell you about my school. I think it would be much more practical if you could see it for yourself. I hope you can visit me as soon as possible.

Sincerely yours,
Susan

44. 重新取得聯繫

親愛的凱文：

　　自從我們國中畢業，你移民之後，時間已過了三年。我很高興能重新跟你取得聯繫，我們一定得好好敘敘舊。你問到關於我的學校生活和社團活動，所以我就跟你說一說吧。

　　當然，你一定記得國中生活的情況。高中生活最大的不同，就在於我們有更大的自由，我們也得擔負更大的責任。老師不再明確地告訴我們要讀什麼，還有何時該唸書，但是我們還是要用功讀書！要得高分的壓力很大。至於社團，我們有很多很好的選擇，那代表我們可以找到一個自己真的很想加入的社團。此外，社團也比較有趣，如果你很努力練習的話，你還可以在正式場合中演出。我今年加入了吉他社，我很喜歡這個社團！

　　我還有很多與學校生活有關的事想跟你說，我覺得你親自來看看可能比較實際些，我希望你能快點來看我。

　　　　　　　　　　　　　　　　　　蘇珊　敬上

**

graduate〔'grædʒʊ,et〕*v.* 畢業
emigrate〔'ɛmə,gret〕*v.* 移民　　***get in touch*** 取得聯繫
catch up on 敘舊　　freedom〔'fridəm〕*n.* 自由
responsibility〔rɪ,spɑnsə'bɪlətɪ〕*n.* 責任
exactly〔ɪg'zæktlɪ〕*adv.* 確切地
pressure〔'prɛʃɚ〕*n.* 壓力　　***as for*** 至於
keen〔kin〕*adj.* 渴望的　　***give a performance*** 表演
formal〔'fɔrml̩〕*adj.* 正式的
occasion〔ə'keʃən〕*n.* 場合　　practice〔'præktɪs〕*v.* 練習
practical〔'præktɪkl̩〕*adj.* 實際的　　***for oneself*** 親自

45. A Letter to a Pen Pal

Dear Derek,

I wanted to share some good news with you. I got accepted into NTU! *This is a dream come true for me.* The last year was very difficult. I studied so hard. Every free moment was dedicated to achieving this goal. *Most importantly*, I could not have done it without your encouragement.

Now that I will attend NTU, I have set some goals. *The first* is to study just as hard and get excellent grades. *The second* is to make new friends and explore new interests. Time is precious. I won't waste a minute of it.

Thank you so much for being in my corner. Your support made all the difference. I wish everyone had a friend like you. Hopefully, I can continue to be successful in college. *I will do my best.*

Sincerely,

Daniel

45. 給筆友的一封信

親愛的德瑞克：

　　我想要跟你分享一些好消息，我考上台大了！這對我來說是夢想成真。去年是非常辛苦的一年，我很用功唸書，每個空閒時刻都致力於達成這目標。最重要的是，沒有你的鼓勵，我無法達成這個目標。

　　既然我要上台大了，我設定了一些目標。首先就是要一樣努力用功，以獲得優異的成績。第二是要交新的朋友和探索新的興趣。時間很寶貴，我不會浪費任何一分鐘。

　　謝謝你這麼支持我，你的支持有很大的影響。我希望每個人都有個跟你一樣的朋友，但願我在大學能持續成功，我會全力以赴的。

　　　　　　　　　　　　　　　　　丹尼爾　敬上

** ————————————————————————

NTU 台大（ = *National Taiwan University* ）
dream come true 美夢成真　　free〔 fri 〕 *adj.* 空閒的
dedicate〔 'dɛdə,ket 〕 *v.* 奉獻；致力於
be dedicated to + V-ing 致力於
achieve〔 ə'tʃiv 〕 *v.* 達到　　goal〔 gol 〕 *n.* 目標
encouragement〔 ɪn'kɝɪdʒmənt 〕 *v.* 鼓勵　　***now that*** 既然
attend〔 ə'tɛnd 〕 *v.* 上（大學）　　set〔 sɛt 〕 *v.* 設定
excellent〔 'ɛksḷənt 〕 *adj.* 優秀的　　explore〔 ɪk'splor 〕 *v.* 探索
precious〔 'prɛʃəs 〕 *adj.* 珍貴的　　***be in one's corner*** 支持某人
support〔 sə'port 〕 *n.* 支持
make all the difference 有很大的差別；有很大的影響
hopefully〔 'hopfəlɪ 〕 *adv.* 有希望地；但願　　***do one's best*** 盡力

46. A Letter to an Ailing Classmate

Dear David,

You haven't been to school since last Monday. Everybody is worried about you. Our teacher told us that you have been infected with H1N1. This is terrible news. *However*, all of us hope you can come back to school as soon as possible. Basketball season has begun and you are the best player on the team. We don't stand a chance without you.

Let me tell you what has happened this week so far. *In the first game*, Jack scored 22 points but he sprained his left ankle. He won't be able to play for two months. *In the second game*, Jared played great defense but the other team still beat us.

Despite our determination to succeed, we aren't doing very well. We really need a leader. *Therefore, we all wish you a speedy recovery*. Come back to school ASAP!

Regards,

Ted

46. 給生病同學的一封信

親愛的大衛：

　　你從上星期一之後，就一直沒來上學。大家都很擔心你。老師告訴我們你感染了新流感。這個消息很嚇人，不過，我們都希望你能儘快回到學校。籃球賽季已經開始了，而你是球隊中最棒的球員。沒有你，我們沒有機會贏。

　　讓我告訴你這星期到目前爲止所發生的事。在第一場比賽，傑克得了 22 分，但卻扭傷了左腳的腳踝。他將有兩個月不能打球。在第二場比賽，傑瑞德防守得很好，但是另一隊還是打敗了我們。

　　儘管我們下定決心要贏，但是表現得並不是很好。我們眞的需要一位領導者。因此，大家都祝你早日康復。儘快回到學校來吧！

　　　　　　　　　　　　　　　　　　　　泰德　敬上

**─────────────────────

ailing〔'elɪŋ〕*adj.* 生病的　　***be worried about*** 擔心
infect〔ɪn'fɛkt〕*v.* 感染　　***H1N1*** 新型流感
terrible〔'tɛrəbḷ〕*adj.* 可怕的　　news〔njuz〕*n.* 消息
as soon as possible 儘快
season〔'sizṇ〕*n.*（社交、戲劇、運動等的）活動時期
basketball season 籃球賽季　　player〔'pleɚ〕*n.* 球員
stand a chance 有（成功的）希望　　***so far*** 到目前爲止
score〔skor〕*v.* 得（分）　　point〔pɔɪnt〕*n.* 分
sprain〔spren〕*v.* 扭傷　　defense〔dɪ'fɛns〕*n.* 防守
determination〔dɪ,tɜmə'neʃən〕*n.* 決心　　***do well*** 表現好
speedy〔'spidɪ〕*adj.* 迅速的　　recovery〔rɪ'kʌvərɪ〕*n.* 康復
ASAP 儘快（= *as soon as possible*）
regards〔rɪ'gɑrdz〕*n. pl.*（書信等的）問候

47. A Letter of Greetings

Dear Mr. and Mrs. Noble,

Has it been a year already? It seems like only yesterday I was there with you in England. Oh how I have missed you! *The memories of my visit stay with me always*.

First, I would like to express my gratitude to you. I couldn't have had better hosts. You made my first visit to a foreign country such a memorable experience. *Second,* thanks for the English lessons! Not only did I learn to communicate with your neighbors, but I am now able to talk to foreigners in my country as well. That's really cool!

Last but not least, I now have a positive outlook on life. Had it not been for the experience in England, I don't know what would have become of me. *It dramatically changed my life for the better*. I don't know how I can ever repay your kindness. Maybe one day you would like to come to Taiwan? It would be my pleasure to be your host.

Sincerely,

Karen

47. 一封問候信

親愛的諾柏先生及諾柏太太：

已經一年了嗎？似乎跟你們在英國的日子才像昨天而已，我真的好想你們！我在英國的回憶一直留在我的腦海裡。

首先，我想要表達對你的感激，你們是最棒的寄宿家庭，你們讓我第一次出國旅行的經驗很難忘。第二，謝謝你們的英文課程！我不僅學會跟你們的鄰居溝通，我現在也能在我的國家跟外國人說話了，那真的很酷！

最後一項要點是，我現在對人生有正面的看法。要不是有在英國的經驗，我不知道我現在會變成怎樣，這次經驗讓我的人生更加美好。我不知道如何報答你們對我的好，說不定有一天你們會想來台灣？能接待你們會是我的榮幸。

凱倫　敬上

** ————————————

greetings〔'gritɪŋz〕*n. pl.* 問候
memory〔'mɛmərɪ〕*n.* 回憶　　express〔ɪk'sprɛs〕*v.* 表達
gratitude〔'grætə,tud〕*n.* 感激
host〔host〕*n.* 主人　　　foreign〔'fɔrɪn〕*adj.* 外國的
memorable〔'mɛmərəbl̩〕*adj.* 難忘的
communicate〔kə'mjumə,ket〕*v.* 溝通
neighbor〔'nebɚ〕*n.* 鄰居　　foreigner〔'fɔrɪnɚ〕*n.* 外國人
as well 也（= *too*）　　**last but not least** 最後一項要點是
positive〔'pazətɪv〕*adj.* 正面的　　outlook〔'aʊt,lʊk〕*n.* 看法
become of …怎麼樣；…遭遇（如何）
dramatically〔drə'mætɪklɪ〕*adv.* 大大地
change ~ for the better 改善～　　repay〔rɪ'pe〕*v.* 報答
kindness〔'kaɪndnɪs〕*n.* 仁慈　　pleasure〔'plɛʒɚ〕*n.* 榮幸

48. A Letter to a Host Family

Dear Host Mom,

My name is Andrew. I come from Taiwan, which used to be called Formosa. That means a beautiful island. I live with my mom, my dad, and my elder brother. My parents often travel to other countries on business. *Thus*, I often hear them talk about many interesting things that happen in different cultures. It is very attractive to me. *Therefore*, I have decided to stay in America for a month.

I'm really looking forward to this homestay experience because I am interested in making friends from different cultures. I think that it could broaden my horizons. *In addition*, I am fascinated by different kinds of food. Every time I go on a trip, I'm always willing to try every local dish even if it is very odd. I think that it is a way for me to experience the real local culture. *I am sure I will have an awesome time for the month I stay with you*.

Sincerely,

Andrew

48. 給寄宿家庭的一封信

親愛的接待媽媽：

　　我的名字是安德魯，我來自台灣，過去被稱爲福爾摩沙，意思是一個美麗的島嶼。我跟我的媽媽、爸爸跟哥哥住在一起，我父母常因公到其他的國家出差，所以我常常會聽他們說一些發生在不同文化的有趣的事，那很吸引我。因此，我決定要在美國住一個月。

　　我眞的很期待這次的寄宿體驗，因爲我對結交來自不同文化的朋友很感興趣，我認爲那可以拓展我的眼界。此外，我也很喜歡各式各樣的食物。每次只要我去旅行，即使當地菜餚很古怪，我總是很願意嘗試，因爲我覺得那是體驗眞實當地文化的方式。我確信這一個月的寄宿體驗會很棒。

安德魯　敬上

** ——————————————————

host family 寄宿家庭　　island（ˈaɪlənd）*n.* 島嶼
on business 因爲公事　　thus（ðʌs）*adv.* 因此
attractive（əˈtræktɪv）*adj.* 吸引人的
look forward to 期待　　*make friends* 交朋友
broaden one's horizons 拓展眼界
fascinate（ˈfæsn̩ˌet）*v.* 使著迷
willing（ˈwɪlɪŋ）*adj.* 願意的
local（ˈlokl̩）*adj.* 當地的　　dish（dɪʃ）*n.* 菜餚
odd（ɑd）*adj.* 奇怪的
awesome（ˈɔsəm）*adj.* 很棒的

49. A Letter to the Beyond

Dear Grandma,

How are you? I hope everything is fine in heaven. It has been a year since you left us. The world is completely different without you. I miss you a lot, especially when I feel upset. You were the one who always cheered me up and got me through the hard times. *Life is hard without your support*, but I am *learning to handle things on my own*.

I have changed a lot. Do you remember that I was always out playing when you were around? And you told me that play is good, but you also wanted me to find out what I really wanted to do with my life. I think I have found it. I have been studying lately because I want to be a doctor. I can still remember clearly the day you passed away. When the doctor said that she couldn't save you because the medical skill today was not enough for you, I was angry and felt helpless. Now *I try really hard to pursue my goal though there are many obstacles*. I have overcome several in the past year, and I am confident that I can get through the rest. I hope everything is great with you too.

Sincerely,

Phil

49.　寄到死後世界的一封信

親愛的奶奶：

　　您好嗎？我希望在天堂的您一切都順利。您離開我們一年了，這個世界因為沒有您而變得完全不同。我很想您，尤其是我傷心時。之前總是您逗我開心，在我困難的時候支持我。沒有您的支持，生活變得很辛苦，但我正在學習如何自己處理事情。

　　我有了很大的改變。您還記得您還在的時候，我很喜歡出門去玩嗎？您告訴我玩樂固然好，但是您也要我找到我人生真正喜愛做的事，我想我已經找到了。我最近都很用功唸書，因為我想成為一名醫生。我仍清楚記得您走的那一天。當醫生說她無法救您，因為現今的醫術還不足以醫治您，我很生氣也覺得很無助。雖然有很多阻礙，但我現在非常努力追求我的目標。過去這一年，我已克服許多困難，我有信心能克服接下來的阻礙，我也希望您一切都安好。

菲爾　敬上

** ─────

the beyond 死後的世界　　heaven〔ˈhɛvən〕*n.* 天堂
completely〔kəmˈplitlɪ〕*adv.* 完全
upset〔ʌpˈsɛt〕*adj.* 難過的　　support〔səˈport〕*n.* 支持
cheer *sb.* ***up*** 使某人振作精神　　handle〔ˈhændḷ〕*v.* 處理
around〔əˈraʊnd〕*adv.* 在周圍；在附近
on *one's* ***own*** 靠自己　　***pass away*** 去世
medical〔ˈmɛdɪkḷ〕*adj.* 醫學的
helpless〔ˈhɛlplɪs〕*adj.* 無助的　　pursue〔pɚˈsu〕*v.* 追求
goal〔gol〕*n.* 目標　　obstacle〔ˈɑbstəkḷ〕*n.* 阻礙
overcome〔ˌovɚˈkʌm〕*v.* 克服
confident〔ˈkɑnfədənt〕*adj.* 有信心的　　***get through*** 克服

50. A Letter to a Friend in France

Dear Lily,

How's everything in France? I want to share an experience that made a good impression on me. I volunteered to work with a charity in southern Taiwan during my winter vacation. We went to the primary schools in remote areas to teach students English.

We played many games, sang English songs, watched English cartoons, and so on. All of us had a fantastic time. *Most important of all*, the students were very hard-working and eager to learn English. *They cherished and appreciated the opportunity to learn a foreign language*. I received many cards made by students. Most of them were very happy with the English lessons and thankful for our efforts.

What also made a good impression on me was the attitude of the students. They cherished everything they had and didn't feel frustrated by their relative poverty. *They tried hard to improve their ability and learn about the world*. Someday, I hope we will have the chance to go together to help people in need. I think the experience will influence us a lot.

Sincerely,
Phil

50. 給法國朋友的一封信

親愛的莉莉：

　　在法國的一切還好嗎？我想跟妳分享一個讓我留下良好印象的經驗。我寒假時在南台灣擔任一個慈善機構的義工。我們到偏遠地區的國小去教學生英文。

　　我們玩了許多遊戲、唱英文歌、看英文卡通等等。我們大家都玩得很開心。最重要的是，學生都很努力，很想學英文，他們很珍惜，也很感激能有機會學習外國語言。我收到很多學生做的卡片，大部分的學生都對這些英文課程很滿意，也很感激我們的努力。

　　還有一個讓我印象深刻的，就是學生的態度。他們很珍惜自己擁有的一切，而且不會因為自身的貧困感到沮喪。他們努力提升自己的能力，並了解這個世界。有朝一日，我希望我們能有機會合作，一起去幫助窮困的人。我覺得這樣的經驗會對我們有很大的影響。

菲爾 敬上

** ─────────────────────────

share〔ʃɛr〕v. 分享　　impression〔ɪmˈprɛʃən〕n. 印象
volunteer〔͵vɑlənˈtɪr〕v. 自願　　charity〔ˈtʃærətɪ〕n. 慈善機構
primary school 小學　　remote〔rɪˈmot〕adj. 遙遠的；偏僻的
and so on 等等　　fantastic〔fænˈtæstɪk〕adj. 很棒的
most important of all 最重要的是　　eager〔ˈigɚ〕adj. 渴望的
cherish〔ˈtʃɛrɪʃ〕v. 珍惜　　appreciate〔əˈpriʃɪ͵et〕v. 感激
opportunity〔͵ɑpɚˈtjunətɪ〕n. 機會　　foreign〔ˈfɔrɪn〕adj. 外國的
be happy with 對～滿意　　thankful〔ˈθæŋkfəl〕adj. 感激的
frustrate〔ˈfrʌstret〕v. 使受挫　　relative〔ˈrɛlətɪv〕adj. 相對的
poverty〔ˈpɑvɚtɪ〕n. 貧窮　　*in need* 在患難中；窮困
influence〔ˈɪnfluəns〕v. 影響

51. A Letter from a Fan

Dear Jeremy Lin,

My name is Jack Lee, and I am one of your biggest fans. I'm crazy about basketball, and I visit your Facebook page every day. I am now writing to you to ask for your approval of my proposal.

I want to establish a fan club for you. You performed a miracle in the NBA and now the whole world is paying attention to what you do and how your performance is. You must be tired sometimes. I want to be the leader of a group of your most devoted fans. *We can cheer you up or give you a hand whenever you need us.*

I'm sure I could do a good job as the leader of your fan club. I have experience in being my class leader, so I know how to motivate people. I think I could take on this job and do it well. *Would you please reply to me when you have a chance?* Thank you for being such a great person.

Sincerely yours,
Jack Lee

51. 一封球迷寫的信

親愛的林書豪：

　　我叫李傑克，我是你最忠實的球迷之一。我熱愛籃球，所以每天都會上你的臉書的網頁。我寫這封信給你，是要請求你同意我的提議。

　　我想爲你成立粉絲俱樂部。你在 NBA 創造了奇蹟，現在全世界都在注意你的一舉一動，看你的表現如何。你一定偶爾會覺得累。我想成爲你最忠實的粉絲團的團長。當你需要我們的時候，我們可以爲你加油打氣，或是幫助你。

　　我相信我能成爲稱職的粉絲團團長。我有當班長的經驗，所以我知道如何激勵大家。我想我可以做這份工作，並且做得很好。可以請你有機會的時候回信給我嗎？謝謝你，你眞的很棒。

李傑克　敬上

**

fan〔fæn〕 *n.* 迷　　***be crazy about*** 很喜歡；很迷戀
visit〔'vɪzɪt〕 *v.* 上（…網站）
Facebook〔'fes,bʊk〕 *n.* 臉書
page〔pedʒ〕 *n.* 網頁　　approval〔ə'pruvḷ〕 *n.* 同意
proposal〔prə'pozḷ〕 *n.* 提議
establish〔ə'stæblɪʃ〕 *v.* 創立
perform a miracle 創造奇蹟（ = *do a miracle* = *work a miracle*)
performance〔pɚ'fɔrməns〕 *n.* 表現
devoted〔dɪ'votɪd〕 *adj.* 忠誠的；狂熱的
cheer *sb.* ***up*** 激勵某人　　***give*** *sb.* ***a hand*** 幫助某人
motivate〔'motə,vet〕 *v.* 激勵
take on 承擔（工作）　　reply〔rɪ'plaɪ〕 *v.* 回覆

52. A Movie Recommendation

Dear Milly,

I want to recommend that you watch a popular and wonderful Taiwanese movie—The Apple's Eye. It is about five teenagers and the girl who all of them have a crush on. It's a true story, and it was written by one of the real boys in the story. This man is now a famous writer in Taiwan. He is also the director of the movie. He wants to tell that girl that he still cherishes the memory of that time.

What's more, this movie takes place in a small village. It brings back a lot of wonderful memories for older people in Taiwan. *The director wants to make everyone in the audience remember his first love and cherish the people around him*.

Love,
Mary

52. 電影推薦

親愛的米莉：

　　我想要推薦妳看一部賣座而且很棒的台灣電影——「那些年，我們一起追的女孩」。這是五個青少年，以及他們所暗戀的一位女孩的故事。這是一個真實的故事，是由故事中的一位男生所演的，這個人現在是台灣一位有名的作家，他也是這部電影的導演。他想要告訴那個女孩，他仍然很珍惜當時的回憶。

　　此外，這部電影的故事發生在一個小村莊，所以喚起了台灣老一輩人的美好回憶。導演的用意是要讓每個觀眾都能記住初戀，以及珍惜身邊的人。

瑪莉　敬上

**

recommendation〔ˌrɛkəmɛn'deʃən〕n. 推薦
recommend〔ˌrɛkə'mɛnd〕v. 推薦
teenager〔'tin,edʒɚ〕n. 青少年
crush〔krʌʃ〕n. 迷戀　***have a crush on*** 迷戀
director〔də'rɛktɚ〕n. 導演
cherish〔'tʃɛrɪʃ〕v. 珍惜
what's more 此外；而且
take place 發生　village〔'vɪlɪdʒ〕n. 村莊
memory〔'mɛmərɪ〕n. 回憶
audience〔'ɔdɪəns〕n. 觀眾　***first love*** 初戀

53. A Reference Letter

Dear Admissions Committee,

I am writing this letter on behalf of one of my best mathematics students, Sean Brown. Mr. Brown is an outstanding student who has always earned excellent grades. *It was no surprise to me when he received a 15 in the math portion of the General Scholastic Ability Test, the highest score possible.* He has been an active and eager learner in my class, and I also know that he has performed extremely well in his other courses. Mr. Brown is not only a hard worker, but also a responsible person. *In addition,* he is well liked by his peers and never hesitates to assist them when they need help.

It is his ambition to enter The Chinese University of Hong Kong. I am sure he would be a positive addition to your student body and would take full advantage the great opportunity to study at your institution. I have no doubt that Mr. Brown will succeed at whatever he pursues in the future. *I hope you will give his application favorable consideration.*

Sincerely,
Tom Smith

53.　一封推薦信

親愛的招生委員：

　　我是爲了我的一位數學很優秀的學生尙恩・布朗而寫這封信。布朗是很傑出的學生，成績一直很好。他學測數學考十五級分，是最高分，我一點也不驚訝。他在我們班上一直很主動又充滿熱誠，我知道其他課程他也表現得很好。史考特不但努力，也很負責任。此外，他深受同儕喜愛，當他們需要幫忙時，他都會毫不猶豫伸出援手。

　　他的目標是要進入香港中文大學就讀，我確定他能成爲貴校優秀的學生，而且會充分利用在貴校就讀的大好機會。我相信布朗未來不論做什麼，都一定會成功。希望你們能同意他的入學申請。

湯姆・史密斯　敬上

＊＊ ─────────────────

reference〔'rɛfərəns〕*n.* 推薦信　　admission〔əd'mɪʃən〕*n.* 入學
admissions committee 招生委員
on behalf of 代表；爲了（= *in behalf of*）
outstanding〔'aut'stændɪŋ〕*adj.* 傑出的　　earn〔ɝn〕*v.* 獲得
scholastic〔skə'læstɪk〕*adj.* 學術的；學習的
possible〔'pasəbḷ〕*adj.*【與最高級連用以加強語氣】可能限度的
active〔'æktɪv〕*adj.* 主動的　　eager〔'igɚ〕*adj.* 熱切的；渴望的
perform〔pɚ'fɔrm〕*v.* 表現
extremely〔ɪk'strimlɪ〕*adv.* 非常　　peer〔pɪr〕*n.* 同儕
hesitate〔'hɛzə,tet〕*v.* 猶豫　　assist〔ə'sɪst〕*v.* 協助
ambition〔æm'bɪʃən〕*n.* 抱負；追求的目標
positive〔'pazətɪv〕*adj.* 正面的；良好的
addition〔ə'dɪʃən〕*n.* 增加物；添加物
body〔'badɪ〕*n.* 團體；群體　　institution〔,ɪnstə'tjuʃən〕*n.* 機構
pursue〔pɚ'su〕*v.* 追求；從事　　favorable〔'fevərəbḷ〕*adj.* 贊同的
favorable consideration 贊同

54. A Letter to the Admissions Board

To Whom It May Concern:

My name is Tim Lee. I am applying to this university. I wish to study computer science. I am a very curious person. I am always asking "Why?" Computer science is full of riddles and problems to solve, and I love finding solutions. *Therefore, I think I would make an excellent candidate for acceptance.*

Computer science is a flourishing industry. The market is always evolving. The future of computer technology is limitless. This is why I really want to get involved. In terms of academic performance, I have excellent grades in math and physics. Both of these subjects will be helpful in my chosen field. With these skills, in combination with my attitude, I know I can go far. *My personal motto is borrowed from Steve Jobs: "Stay hungry, stay foolish."*

I hope you will give me due consideration for acceptance to your school. *I know I will be a positive addition to the student body.*

Best wishes,
Tim Lee

54. 給入學委員會的一封信

敬啓者：

　　我的名字叫李提姆，我要申請貴大學，我希望能就讀資訊工程學系。我生性好奇，我總是會問「爲什麼？」資訊工程充滿了難解的謎以及有待解決的問題，而且我又很喜歡尋找解答。因此，我認爲我能成爲錄取的絕佳人選。

　　資訊工程是個蓬勃發展的產業，市場一直不斷在演變，電腦科技的未來不可限量，所以我眞的很想參與其中。就學術的表現而言，我的數學以及物理成績優異，這兩個科目對我所選擇的領域而言會很有幫助。有了這些專業技術，再加上我的態度，我知道我能有不錯的表現。我個人的座右銘借自史提夫・賈伯斯：「求知若渴，虛懷若谷。」

　　我希望你們能認眞考慮是否要錄取我就讀貴校。我知道我能讓貴校多一位優秀的學生。

　　　　　　　　　　　　　　　寄上由衷的祝福，
　　　　　　　　　　　　　　　李提姆

** ————————————

admission〔əd'mɪʃən〕*n.* 入學　　board〔bord〕*n.* 委員會
computer science 資訊工程
optimistic〔ˌɑptə'mɪstɪk〕*adj.* 樂觀的
riddle〔'rɪdḷ〕*n.* 謎　　solution〔sə'luʃən〕*n.* 解決之道
make〔mek〕*v.* 成爲　　candidate〔'kændə͵det〕*n.* 候選人
flourishing〔'flɝɪʃɪŋ〕*adj.* 繁榮的　　industry〔'ɪndəstrɪ〕*n.* 產業
evolve〔ɪ'vɑlv〕*v.* 演變　　involved〔ɪn'vɑlvd〕*adj.* 有關連的
in terms of 從…的觀點來看　　academic〔͵ækə'dɛmɪk〕*adj.* 學術的
performance〔pɚ'fɔrməns〕*n.* 表現　　field〔fild〕*n.* 領域
in combination with 加上　　*go far* 表現好（= *do well*）
motto〔'mɑto〕*n.* 座右銘　　due〔du〕*adj.* 適當的
due consideration 充分的考慮　　positive〔'pɑzətɪv〕*adj.* 正面的
addition〔ə'dɪʃən〕*n.* 增加物　　body〔'bɑdɪ〕*n.* 群體；團體

55. A Letter to a Foreign Official

Dear President Smith,

My name is Jack Lee and I am a Taiwanese student. I recently read an article which said your country is thinking about granting visa-free status to Taiwan. Here's why I think that's an excellent idea.

First, it's good for business. It will boost your country's tourism sector. Taiwanese people love to travel. *Your country is our number one most popular destination*. With visa-free status, you would soon see a wave of Taiwanese rushing to visit your beautiful country. *Second*, Taiwanese are very nice people. We have great respect for other cultures. *Therefore*, we make excellent guests. *Finally*, it would certainly be a benefit to me! My dream is to study at a university in your country. *A change in the law could make my dream come true*.

Thank you for your time. I realize you are a busy man. *However*, I really hope you make a decision in Taiwan's favor.

Sincerely,
Jack Lee

55. 給外國官員的一封信

親愛的史密斯總統：

　　我的名字是李傑克，我是一名台灣學生。我最近讀到一篇文章，上頭說貴國正在考慮給予台灣免簽證的優惠。以下就是爲什麼我會覺得那是一個很棒的主意。

　　首先，這對商業有益，可以振興貴國的旅遊業。台灣人喜愛旅遊，貴國是最受我們台灣人歡迎的旅遊目的地。因爲免簽證的關係，您將很快見到一群台灣人湧入，參訪您美麗的國家。第二，台灣人民善良，我們很尊敬其它的文化，因此，我們是很棒的客人。最後，對我來說一定是有益的！我的夢就是要到貴國就讀大學，法規上的改變可使我夢想成眞。

　　謝謝您撥冗讀這封信，我知道您很忙碌，但是我眞的很希望您能做出對台灣有利的決定。

　　　　　　　　　　　　　　　　李傑克　敬上

**

foreign〔ˈfɔrɪn〕*adj.* 外國的　　official〔əˈfɪʃəl〕*n.* 官員
recently〔ˈrisn̩tlɪ〕*adv.* 最近　　article〔ˈɑrtɪkl̩〕*n.* 文章
grant〔grænt〕*v.* 給予　　visa〔ˈvizə〕*n.* 簽證
free〔fri〕*adj.* 免除…的　　status〔ˈstetəs〕*n.* 狀態；地位；身分
boost〔bust〕*v.* 提高；推動；促進
tourism〔ˈturɪzəm〕*n.* 觀光　　sector〔ˈsɛktɚ〕*n.* 部門
destination〔ˌdɛstəˈneʃən〕*n.* 目的地；景點
a wave of 一波；一群　　rush〔rʌʃ〕*v.* 蜂湧
respect〔rɪˈspɛkt〕*n.* 尊敬；尊重　　make〔mek〕*v.* 成爲
excellent〔ˈɛksl̩ənt〕*adj.* 極好的　　guest〔gɛst〕*n.* 客人
benefit〔ˈbɛnəfɪt〕*n.* 好處；利益　　realize〔ˈriəˌlaɪz〕*v.* 了解
in one's favor 對…有益

56. A Volunteer Position

Dear Mr. Clement,

I am writing to you about the volunteer positions at the hospital. I know that there are only a few positions left, and I hope that you will choose me for one of them. I really want to be a volunteer in the hospital because I am interested in helping people. I have also read a lot of books about psychology, so I think I can understand how the patients feel. *But the most important thing is that* I am enthusiastic. *I really want to help people who are in need!*

When I was little, my mother fell down and broke her leg. While she stayed in the hospital, there was a volunteer who helped her and talked to her. Thanks to that volunteer, my mother could pass the time more happily. I admired the volunteer then, and I would like to do something similar. *I promise that I will be one of your most dedicated and responsible helpers.* Please give me a chance. Thank you.

Sincerely,
Phil Lee

56. 義工的職務

親愛的克萊門先生：

　　我寫這封信給你的目的，是關於醫院義工的職務的問題。我知道職位所剩無幾，所以我希望您能錄取我。我眞的很想擔任醫院裡的義工，因爲我很喜歡幫助別人。我也讀過許多心理學方面的書，所以我想我能體會病人的感受，但最重要的是，我很有熱忱，我眞的很想幫助需要幫助的人！

　　當我還很小的時候，我的母親跌倒摔斷了腿。在她住院的時候，有一位義工幫助她，而且還跟她說話。多虧有那位義工，所以我的母親才可以愉快地度過那段時間。那時我很欽佩那位義工，也希望能做類似的事。我保證我會成爲醫院中最認眞、而且最負責任的義工之一。請給我一次機會，謝謝。

李菲爾　敬上

** ────────────

volunteer〔ˌvɑlən'tɪr〕*n.* 自願者；義工

position〔pə'zɪʃən〕*n.* 職位　　left〔lɛft〕*adj.* 剩下的

be interested in 對…感興趣

psychology〔saɪ'kɑlədʒɪ〕*n.* 心理學

patient〔'peʃənt〕*n.* 病人　　***in need*** 需要幫助的；窮困的

fall down 跌倒　　stay〔ste〕*v.* 暫住

thanks to 幸虧；因爲　　pass〔pæs〕*v.* 度過（時間）

admire〔əd'maɪr〕*v.* 欽佩　　***would like to + V.*** 想要～

similar〔'sɪmələ〕*adj.* 類似的

promise〔'prɑmɪs〕*v.* 保證

dedicated〔'dɛdəˌketɪd〕*adj.* 專注的

helper〔'hɛlpə〕*n.* 幫手

57. Going to the Olympics

Dear Ms. Smith,

I have heard the news that you want more international volunteers for the Olympics. *I can't tell you how much I would love to take part.* I want to participate in the Olympics not only because I admire the event and the athletes that compete in it, but also because I have dreamed of visiting your beautiful city for many years.

I believe I could work well as a volunteer because I have been preparing for it for a long time. Since I heard the news, I had been working at a part-time job to earn enough money to afford the trip. *Besides,* I'm not only good at English but also two other languages. *I love to interact with people and am willing to help.* All I need is for you to give me a chance. So please don't turn down my request to be a volunteer at the Olympics.

Sincerely,
Phil Lee

57. 來去奧林匹克

親愛的史密斯小姐：

　　我聽說你們奧林匹克運動會需要更多國際義工，我真的無法表達我有多想參加。我想參加奧運，不只是因為我很欽佩奧林匹克運動會，以及參加競賽的運動員，而且還因為我已經夢想拜訪你們美麗的城市好多年了。

　　我相信我可以勝任義工這個工作，因為我已經準備了好長一段時間。自從我聽到這個消息，我就一直在兼差賺取這趟行程的旅費。另外，我不僅英文好，其他兩個語言也很好。我喜歡跟其他人互動，也願意幫助大家。我所需要的就是你們能給我一個機會。所以請不要拒絕我想當奧林匹克運動會義工的請求。

　　　　　　　　　　　李菲爾　敬上

** ————————————————

the Olympics　奧林匹克運動會（= *the Olympic Games*）
international〔͵ɪntɚˋnæʃən̩〕*adj.* 國際的
volunteer〔͵vɑlənˋtɪr〕*n.* 自願者；義工
take part　參加　　participate〔pɑrˋtɪsə͵pet〕*v.* 參加
admire〔ədˋmaɪr〕*v.* 欽佩　　event〔ɪˋvɛnt〕*n.* 大型活動
athlete〔ˋæθlit〕*n.* 運動員　　compete〔kəmˋpit〕*v.* 競爭
dream of　夢想　　***work as***　擔任
part-time〔ˋpɑrtˋtaɪm〕*adj.* 兼職的
afford〔əˋford〕*v.* 負擔　　***be good at***　擅長
interact〔͵ɪntɚˋækt〕*v.* 互動　　***be willing to***　願意
turn down　拒絕　　request〔rɪˋkwɛst〕*n.* 請求；要求

58. Recommending a Book

Dear Tom,

I'd like to share an interesting book with you. It's called *Helen Keller*. Old as the story may be, it is still very popular. The new edition is selling like hotcakes— maybe even better than *Harry Potter*. The book is about Helen's amazing and inspiring life. Born healthy, she suffered a childhood illness that left her deaf and blind. *Fortunately,* Helen met a teacher who encouraged her to live a normal life. Thanks to a supportive family, after a long struggle, Helen finally achieved success. She went on to become a very famous woman.

Tom, I know that you are facing some difficulties right now. Perhaps you are afraid of taking action for fear of making a mistake. Maybe if you read the book it will give you strength and courage to take some risks. *Otherwise, opportunities will slip through your fingers.*

Just as the Indian poet Tagore said, "If you shed tears when you miss the sun, you also miss the stars." *I hope that this book will inspire you to follow your dreams.* Don't give up!

Sincerely yours,
Harry

58. 推薦一本書

親愛的湯姆：

　　我想跟你分享一本有趣的書，書名是海倫凱勒。雖然這個故事流傳已久，但是還是很受歡迎。新的版本非常暢銷，可能比哈利波特還暢銷。這本書述說海倫凱勒不尋常且激勵人心的生命過程。她出生時很健康，但是歷經一場孩提時代的重病，讓她又聾又瞎。海倫凱勒有幸遇到一位鼓勵她過正常生活的老師，而且有一個支持她的家庭，在奮鬥許久後，海倫凱勒終於成功了，她後來就成為一位非常有名的人。

　　湯姆，我知道現在你正面臨一些困難，或許你因為害怕犯錯，而不敢採取行動。或許讀完這本書之後，你能有勇氣去冒險犯難。否則，機會會從你的指間溜走。

　　就像印度詩人泰戈爾說的：「如果你因為錯過太陽而流淚，那你也將錯過群星。」我希望這本書能激勵你追求你的夢想。不要放棄！

亨利　敬上

** ──────────────

recommend〔͵rɛkə'mɛnd〕v. 推薦
edition〔ɪ'dɪʃən〕n. 版本　　　***sell like hotcakes*** 熱銷
amazing〔ə'mezɪŋ〕adj. 驚人的
inspiring〔ɪn'spaɪrɪŋ〕adj. 激勵人心的
suffer〔'sʌfɚ〕v. 受…之苦
leave〔liv〕v. 使處於（某種狀態）
encourage〔ɪn'kɝɪdʒ〕v. 鼓勵　　normal〔'nɔrml̩〕adj. 正常的
thanks to 由於　　supportive〔sə'portɪv〕adj. 有支持力的
struggle〔'stʌgl̩〕n. 奮鬥；努力　　achieve〔ə'tʃiv〕v. 達成
take action 採取行動　　***for fear of*** 害怕
take a risk 冒險　　slip〔slɪp〕v. 溜走
shed〔ʃɛd〕v. 流（淚）　　inspire〔ɪn'spaɪr〕v. 激勵

59. A Most Special Volunteer

Dear Ms. Lee,

I am writing this on behalf of Class 303. Now it is time for us to graduate. But before waving good-bye to senior high school, we want to express our appreciation to you. A lot has happened over these last three years. No other volunteer was quite as special. You were always there for us. You always greeted us with a smile. *Whenever we asked for help, you always came to our aid*.

I remember a scary moment in our second year. David was badly injured during recess. It looked like he had broken his leg. He couldn't walk. None of us knew what to do. *However,* you took charge and drove him to the nearest hospital. What was even more special is what happened next. You drove David home after he received medical attention. Without your help, David may not have been able to recover from the injury. This is just one example of your care. Though you never said "I love you" to us, we all knew that you did!

As graduation is upon us, we want to show our gratitude. We would like to invite you to party in your honor. It's our way of saying thanks for everything

Sincerely yours,

Zoe

59. 一個非常特別的志工

親愛的李小姐：

　　我謹代表 303 班寫這封信。我們現在快要畢業了，但在揮別高中生活之前，我們想要向妳表達感謝。過去三年發生了很多事情，沒有任何志工像妳這麼特別。妳總是隨時幫助我們。妳總是用微笑和我們打招呼。每當我們要求幫助時，妳總是會來幫忙我們。

　　我記得高二時那個令人恐懼的一刻。大衛在下課時受重傷，看似腿骨折了。他無法走路，我們都不知道該怎麼辦。然而，妳擔起責任開車送他去最近的醫院。接下來所發生的事更特別。在大衛接受醫療後，妳又載他回家。沒有妳的幫助，大衛可能無法恢復健康。這只是妳照顧我們的一個例子。雖然妳從未對我們說「我愛你們」，我們都知道妳是愛我們的！

　　畢業將至，我們想要表達對妳的謝意。為了向妳致意，我們想邀請妳參加派對。這是我們表達感謝的方法！

　　　　　　　　　　　　　　　　　　　　　柔伊 敬上

** ————————————————

on behalf of 代表　　*wave goodbye to* 向…揮手告別
appreciation〔əˌpriʃɪˋeʃən〕*n.* 感謝
volunteer〔ˌvɑlənˋtɪr〕*n.* 志工　　greet〔grit〕*v.* 向…問候
aid〔ed〕*n.* 幫助；援助　　*come to one's aid* 來幫助某人
scary〔ˋskɛrɪ〕*adj.* 可怕的　　*be badly injured* 受重傷
recess〔rɪˋsɛs〕*n.* 休息時間　　*take charge* 負責
drive sb. to 開車載某人去…　　*medical attention* 醫療照顧
medical attention 醫療照顧
recover〔rɪˋkʌvə〕*v.* 恢復；康復
care〔kɛr〕*n.* 照顧　　*be upon sb.* 近在咫尺；即將來臨
in one's honor 向…致意；紀念…

60.　An Invitation to a Beach Party

Dear friends,

　　I will be eighteen years old in two weeks. I hope you can come to celebrate and have fun with me. At the party, there will be a barbecue, juice, and a cake. My parents have also invited a band to play music at the party. *We can enjoy the music, sing and dance together. Best of all,* this party is going to be held on the beach! We can rent surfboards and try our skill on the waves, or we can just swim and play on the beach. There will be a volleyball and net if you want to have a game. You can even bury me in the sand if you want, but maybe that's not such a good idea. Ha ha.

　　Anyway, I hope you all can come. The party will be Saturday, May 15. We will meet at my house at 1:00 and then drive to the beach. We will leave the beach after sunset, around 7 pm. Please let me know if you can come by May 12th. That way we can arrange enough cars to take us all there. *I'm really looking forward to it, and I hope you are too!*

　　　　　　　　　　　　　　　Sincerely yours,

　　　　　　　　　　　　　　　Debby

60. 海灘派對邀請函

親愛的朋友：

　　再過兩週我就十八歲了，我希望你們能來慶祝以及與我同樂。在派對上，會有烤肉、果汁以及蛋糕，我的父母也邀請了一個樂團來派對演奏，我們可以享受音樂，一起唱歌跳舞。最棒的是，派對是在沙灘上舉行！我們可以租衝浪板，在浪上試試新技巧，要不然游泳或是在沙灘上玩也可以，想打排球的話，會有一個排球跟網子。如果你們想要的話，也可以把我埋在沙堆裡，可是好像不太好，哈哈。

　　總之，我希望你們都能來。派對日期是五月十五日星期六，我們一點在我家碰面，然後再開車到海灘，我們大概晚上七點，太陽下山後的時間離開沙灘。請在五月十二日之前讓我知道你們要不要來，那樣我們才可以安排足夠的車載大家過去。我真的很期待，希望你們也一樣！

黛比　敬上

＊＊ ─────────────

celebrate〔'sɛlə,bret〕v. 慶祝　　***have fun*** 玩得愉快

barbecue〔'bɑrbɪ,kju〕n. 烤肉　　juice〔dʒus〕n. 果汁

hold〔hold〕v. 舉行　　rent〔rɛnt〕v. 租

surfboard〔'sɜf,bord〕n. 衝浪板

volleyball〔'vɑlɪ,bɔl〕n. 排球　　net〔nɛt〕n. 網

game〔gem〕n. 比賽　　bury〔'bɛrɪ〕v. 埋

anyway〔'ɛnɪ,we〕adv. 無論如何；反正

sunset〔'sʌn,sɛt〕n. 日落　　***that way*** 那樣

arrange〔ə'rendʒ〕v. 安排　　***look forward to*** 期待

61. An Invitation

Dear David,

It's been a while since I last saw you. I hope you are doing well. There is a big event coming up at my school. We are having a carnival to celebrate the school's anniversary. Ming Shan High School is going to be fifty years old! I can hardly believe it.

I think the carnival is going to be a lot of fun. There will be a lot of food for sale, including your favorite, hamburgers. There will also be a talent show and lots of games. Both students and teachers can play the games, and we might even win a prize.

The carnival is open to everyone, so you don't have to be a Ming Shan student to go. I hope that you can go with me. I think we would have a great time. Please let me know as soon as possible. The carnival will be this Saturday.

Your friend,

Ben

61. 一封邀請函

親愛的大衛：

　　好久不見了。我希望你一切都好。我們學校即將會有一個大型活動。我們要舉行園遊會來慶祝校慶。明山高中就要滿五十週年了！我真不敢相信。

　　我想園遊會一定很好玩。會賣很多食物，包括你最喜歡的漢堡。也會有才藝表演和很多遊戲。學生和老師都能玩遊戲，我們還可能會得獎。

　　園遊會大家都可以參加，所以你不必是明山高中的學生也可以去。我希望你能和我一起去。我認為我們會玩得很愉快。請盡快讓我知道。園遊會的時間是這個星期六。

你的朋友，
班

**

invitation〔ˌɪnvə'teʃən〕*n.* 邀請函
a while 一會兒；一段時間
do〔du〕*v.* 進展　　event〔ɪ'vɛnt〕*n.* 事件；大型活動
come up 發生　　have〔hæv〕*v.* 舉行
carnival〔'kɑrnəvḷ〕*n.* 嘉年華會
anniversary〔ˌænə'vɝsərɪ〕*n.* 週年紀念
fun〔fʌn〕*n.* 樂趣；有趣　　***for sale*** 出售的
favorite〔'fevərɪt〕*n.* 最喜歡的人或物
talent show 才藝表演　　prize〔praɪz〕*n.* 獎；獎品
open〔'opən〕*adj.* 開放的　　***have a great time*** 玩得很愉快
as soon as possible 盡快

62. **An Invitation to a Holiday Party**

Dear Helen,

How have you been? I have been busy at school. We are preparing for the Christmas party. It has been difficult. We have faced many obstacles. Who knew planning a party would be so hard? *Anyway,* I really hope you will attend. It will be held at the tennis court at Bo Lin High School. The date is December 24th. The time is 7:00 p.m.

There are plenty of reasons you should come. *First,* there will be tons of food. We will prepare many mouth-watering dishes. There will be many elaborate desserts. I know you have a sweet tooth, so you shouldn't miss out. *Second,* we have invited several special guests. Some of them may surprise you. *Last but not least,* you have to see our giant Christmas tree. My classmates and I spent many hours decorating it with candy and ornaments.

Again, I really hope you come. *Don't give it a second thought. Mark it down on your calendar.* You won't be disappointed.

Sincerely,
Kathy

62. 假日派對邀請函

親愛的海倫：

　　妳好嗎？我在學校一直很忙。我們正在準備聖誕派對，真是不容易，我們遭遇了許多阻礙。誰知道籌劃一場派對會這麼難？不管怎樣，我真的希望妳能參加。聖誕派對會在伯霖高中的網球場舉辦，日期是 12 月 24 日，時間是晚上七點。

　　妳應該來的理由有很多。首先，會有很多食物。我們會準備許多令人垂涎的菜餚。也會有很多精緻的甜點。我知道妳喜歡吃甜食，所以妳不該錯過這次機會。第二，我們邀請了一些特別來賓，有些可能會使妳很驚訝。最後一項要點是，妳一定要看看我們巨大的聖誕樹。我的同學和我花了好幾個小時，用糖果和裝飾品來佈置這棵聖誕樹。

　　而且我真的希望妳能來，不要再考慮了，把它記在妳的行事曆上，妳不會失望的。

凱西　敬上

**

obstacle〔ˈɑbstəkḷ〕*n.* 阻礙；障礙

anyway〔ˈɛnɪˌwe〕*adv.* 不管怎樣；無論如何

attend〔əˈtɛnd〕*v.* 參加　　hold〔hold〕*v.* 舉行

tennis court 網球場　　***plenty of*** 很多的　　***tons of*** 大量的

mouth-watering〔ˈmaʊθˌwɔtərɪŋ〕*adj.* 令人垂涎的

dish〔dɪʃ〕*n.* 菜餚　　elaborate〔ɪˈlæbərɪt〕*adj.* 精緻的

dessert〔dɪˈzɝt〕*n.* 甜點　　***have a sweet tooth*** 喜歡甜食

miss out 錯過機會　　***last but not least*** 最後一項要點是

giant〔ˈdʒaɪənt〕*adj.* 巨大的　　decorate〔ˈdɛkəˌret〕*v.* 裝飾

ornament〔ˈɔrnəmənt〕*n.* 裝飾品

again〔əˈgɛn〕*adv.* 此外；而且　　***a second thought*** 重新考慮

mark down 寫下；記入　　calendar〔ˈkæləndɚ〕*n.* 日曆；日程表

63. The Hare Challenges the Tortoise to a Rematch

Dear Tortoise,

Congratulations! You defeated me last time. *Due to my arrogance, I didn't take the race seriously.* I did not believe you were a worthy opponent. I even fell asleep under a tree. When I woke up, I found you had already arrived at the finish line. *However,* you didn't win the race, tortoise; I lost by being careless. Is that the kind of victory you want?

I hereby challenge you to another race. And this time, I have made up my mind to defeat you. *I will have my revenge.* If you reject this offer, everyone will know you got lucky last time. If you are confident in your abilities, you must accept my offer. Let us have a true competition. Then we shall see who is faster: The Tortoise or the Hare.

So next Monday, same time, same place? See you then.

Sincerely,

Hare

63. 兔子再次找烏龜賽跑

親愛的烏龜：

　　恭喜你！你上次打敗了我。因為我太自大，所以並沒有把比賽看得很認真。我當時不相信你是個勢均力敵的對手。我甚至在樹下睡著了。當我醒來時，發現你已經抵達終點。不過，烏龜，你並沒有贏得比賽；我會輸是因為不小心。你要的就是那樣的勝利嗎？

　　因此我要向你挑戰，我們再比一次。這一次，我已經下定決心要打敗你。我會復仇。如果你拒絕這個提議，大家都會知道你上次只是運氣好。如果你對自己的能力有信心，就必須接受我的提議。讓我們來進行一場真正的比賽吧，然後我們就能知道誰比較快：烏龜還是兔子。

　　所以是下星期一，同樣時間，同樣地點嗎？到時候見。

　　　　　　　　　　　　　　　　　　　　　兔子　敬上

** ───────────────

hare〔hɛr〕*n.* 野兔　　challenge〔'tʃælɪndʒ〕*v.* 向…挑戰
tortoise〔'tɔrtəs〕*n.* 陸龜【turtle〔'tɝtl̩〕*n.* 海龜】
rematch〔'ri,mætʃ〕*n.* 重賽；複賽　　defeat〔dɪ'fit〕*v.* 打敗
due to 由於　　arrogance〔'ærəgəns〕*n.* 自大；傲慢
take sth. seriously 把某事看得很認真
worthy〔'wɝθɪ〕*adj.* 值得的；勢均力敵的
opponent〔ə'ponənt〕*n.* 對手　　*finish line* 終點線
race〔res〕*n.* 賽跑；競賽　　careless〔'kɛrlɪs〕*adj.* 粗心的
victory〔'vɪktrɪ〕*n.* 勝利　　hereby〔,hɪr'baɪ〕*adv.* 藉此；特此
make up one's mind 下定決心　　*have one's revenge* 報仇
reject〔rɪ'dʒɛkt〕*v.* 拒絕　　offer〔'ɔfɚ〕*n.* 提議
confident〔'kɑnfədənt〕*adj.* 有信心的
competition〔,kɑmpə'tɪʃən〕*n.* 競爭；比賽　　see〔si〕*v.* 知道

64. Come Visit Taiwan

Dear Rob,

How's it going? I'd like to invite you to spend a wonderful holiday in Taiwan this summer. We have been pen pals for more than six years now, and we've never met! Isn't it time we got to know each other?

We are both becoming college students this year. I think it will be great if we can spend some time together. *What's more*, you have said that you want to try scuba diving. As you may know, magnificent coral reefs can be found in Taiwan. I really hope you take me up on my offer.

If you come, you can stay at my place, so you do not have to pay for your accommodation. We can start from the northern part of Taiwan and go down south to do the scuba diving. A lot of my other friends can join us on the trip. I am sure you will have fun. *We can try all the traditional Taiwanese dishes and meet many kind and friendly local people*. Let's have a fantastic holiday this summer!

Sincerely yours,

Allen

64. 來台灣玩

親愛的羅伯：

　　最近好嗎？我想邀請你今年夏天來台灣度過一個美妙的假期。我們已經當了六年多的筆友，但是我們竟然沒見過面！我們是不是該見面彼此認識一下呢？

　　我們今年都要上大學了。我想如果我們能聚一聚應該很棒。此外，你說你想要試試水肺潛水，你應該知道在台灣可以找到美麗的珊瑚礁。我真的很希望你能接受我的提議。

　　如果你來的話，可以住在我家，所以你就不用花住宿費。我們可以從北台灣開始，然後南下去潛水。我很多其他的朋友也可以加入我們，我保證你一定會玩得很愉快。我們可以品嚐所有傳統的台灣菜，並且認識許多友善熱情的當地人。就讓我們今年夏天有個很棒的假期吧！

艾倫　敬上

**

spend〔spɛnd〕v. 度過　　***pen pal*** 筆友
get to V. 得以⋯　　***what's more*** 此外
magnificent〔mæg'nɪfəsn̩t〕adj. 壯麗的
scuba diving 水肺潛水　　coral〔'kɔrəl〕n. 珊瑚
reef〔rif〕n. 礁　　***coral reef*** 珊瑚礁
offer〔'ɔfɚ〕n. 提議
take sb. up on sb.'s offer 接受某人的提議
stay〔ste〕v. 暫住　　place〔ples〕n. 住所
accommodations〔ə,kɑmə'deʃənz〕n. pl. 住宿
down south 向南方；在南方　　***have fun*** 玩得愉快
traditional〔trə'dɪʃənl̩〕adj. 傳統的
dish〔dɪʃ〕n. 菜餚　　local〔'lokl̩〕adj. 當地的
fantastic〔fæn'tæstɪk〕adj. 很棒的

65. Inviting a Teacher to a Class Reunion

Dear Mr. Smith,

It has been three years since my class graduated from high school. Those certainly were good times. We have such good memories. You were our greatest support. Our experience was shaped by your care. You were as much a part of high school as our studies. *Everyone thinks the world of you.*

To show our gratitude for all you have done, we'd like to invite you to our reunion. I would like to personally show my appreciation. I really hope that you will come. During high school, it was you who cheered me up when I was down. When I was ready to give up, it was your encouragement that kept me going. *I don't know what would have become of me if not for your guidance.*

The reunion will be held on Friday at the Starbucks in Taipei Main Station. Feel free to call me if you have questions. This will be our chance to say "Thank you." We really hope you come!

Sincerely,

Ken Lee

65. 邀請老師來同學會

親愛的史密斯老師：

　　我們班高中畢業三年了，那段時光眞美妙，我們滿是美好的回憶。您那時是我們最大的支持，我們的高中生活體驗深受您細心呵護的影響。您就跟學校課業一般，是我們高中生活的一部份，每個人都很敬重您。

　　爲了對您爲我們所做的一切表示感謝，我們想邀請您來參加我們的同學會。我想要親自表示我的感激，我眞的很希望您會來，高中時，都是您在我情緒低落時激勵我。當我想要放棄時，是您的鼓勵讓我堅持下去。我不知道如果沒有您的指導，我會變成怎麼樣。

　　同學會舉行的時間是星期五，在台北火車站的星巴克。如果您有任何疑問，歡迎隨時打電話給我。這是一次我們向您說「謝謝」的機會，我們眞的希望您能出席！

李肯　敬上

** ————————————————

reunion〔rɪ'junjən〕*n.* 團聚
class reunion 同學會　　graduate〔'grædʒʊˌet〕*v.* 畢業
support〔sə'port〕*n.* 支持　　shape〔ʃep〕*v.* 塑造
care〔kɛr〕*n.* 關心　　studies〔'stʌdɪz〕*n. pl.* 課業
think the world of 看重　　gratitude〔'grætəˌtud〕*n.* 感激
personally〔'pɝsn̩lɪ〕*adv.* 親自
appreciation〔əˌpriʃɪ'eʃən〕*n.* 感激
cheer sb. up 激勵某人　　down〔daʊn〕*adj.* 心情不好的
give up 放棄　　encouragement〔ɪn'kɝɪdʒmənt〕*n.* 鼓勵
become of …變成（怎麼樣）　　guidance〔'gaɪdn̩s〕*n.* 指導
hold〔hold〕*v.* 舉辦　　*feel free to V.* 可以隨意…

66. A Letter of Condolence

Dear Anna,

I'm so sorry to hear about your father's death. This is a hard time for you. All of us have you and your family in our hearts. Perhaps I can give you some comfort. Your father was a great man. His books encouraged many people to fight depression. You should be proud of your father. He fought the cancer like a warrior. He continued to help others all the way until the very end. *I know how much he meant to you*. We will all miss him.

However, I can't bear to see you so depressed. It's over. He's gone. *Now it is time for you to move on*. This is something I learned from your father. It will help you get back to normal. *First*, you have to stay healthy. *Therefore*, eat right, exercise regularly and get proper rest. *Second*, read your dad's books again. Read how he consoled his readers. *Finally*, talk with your mother more. She is also very sad now. It will comfort you to be with close family members.

If there is anything you need, please let me know. *I am always here for you*, *no matter what*. *If you need to talk*, *cry*, *or just have a laugh*, *just call*.

Best wishes,
Jerry

66. 一封弔唁信

親愛的安娜：

　　聽到妳父親過世的消息，我很遺憾。妳一定覺得很難受。我們都很關心妳和妳的家人。或許我可以給妳一點安慰。妳父親是很棒的人，他寫的書鼓勵很多人對抗憂鬱症，妳應該以妳父親為榮。他像個勇士對抗癌症，持續幫助他人一路到最後。我知道他對妳而言意義重大，我們都會很想念他。

　　然而，看到妳意志如此消沈，令我無法忍受。一切都結束了，他已離開人世，現在是妳該繼續往前進的時候了。這是我從妳父親身上學到的。這能幫助妳回復正常的生活。首先，妳必須保持健康，因此，妳要飲食正常，規律運動，並有適當的休息。第二，再讀一遍妳父親的書。看看他是如何安慰他的讀者。最後，多跟妳的母親聊一聊，她現在也很難過，和妳親近的家人在一起，可以給妳一些安慰。

　　如果妳有任何需要，請讓我知道。無論如何，我永遠支持妳。如果妳需要講話、哭訴，或者想大笑，就打電話給我。

寄上最誠摯的祝福，
傑瑞

**

condolence〔kənˋdoləns〕n. 弔唁；弔慰；哀悼
hard time 艱難時期　　comfort〔ˋkʌmfət〕n. 安慰
fight〔faɪt〕v. 對抗　　depression〔dɪˋprɛʃən〕n. 沮喪；憂鬱症
warrior〔ˋwɔrɪə〕n. 戰士；勇士
all the way until the very end 一直到最後
mean〔min〕v. 有重要性　　bear〔bɛr〕v. 忍受
depressed〔dɪˋprɛst〕adj. 沮喪的　　**move on** 繼續前進
proper〔ˋprɑpə〕adj. 適當的　　normal〔ˋnɔrml̩〕n. 常態
console〔kənˋsol〕v. 安慰
no matter what 不管發生什麼事　　**have a laugh** 大笑

67. Cheering Up a Friend

Dear Lucy,

I know you are in a bad mood because of your test score yesterday. That's natural. *After all*, everyone wants to get a good grade, right? *I understand how you feel, but it's not the end of the world.* Try to see this failure as an opportunity. Think about how you can change your study habits and do better next time. *However*, before you do that, it's important to change your mood. You need to relax and forget about your stress.

How about going for a bike ride on the beach this weekend? There are many beautiful things to see along the way. We can take pictures and swim. It will also be a great way to stretch your arms, legs, and brain. I guarantee that you will feel better afterward. *Let's meet at 10:00 on Saturday.* See you then!

Your friend,
Debby

67. 激勵朋友

親愛的露西：

　　我知道妳因為昨天的考試成績，所以心情不好。那是當然的。畢竟，大家都想得到好成績，不是嗎？我知道妳的感受，但這並不是世界末日。要試著把這次的失敗看作是一個機會。想想看要如何改變妳的讀書習慣，下次才能考得更好。不過，在妳那樣做之前，要先改變妳的心情，這是很重要的。妳必須放鬆，並且忘掉妳的壓力。

　　這個週末一起去海邊騎腳踏車如何？沿途可以看到很多漂亮的東西。我們可以拍照和游泳。這也是個伸展手、腳，以及頭腦很棒的方式。我保證騎完之後，妳一定會覺得好多了。我們就約星期六早上十點吧。到時候見！

　　　　　　　　　　　　　　　　　　妳的朋友，
　　　　　　　　　　　　　　　　　　黛比

**

mood〔mud〕*n.* 心情　　***be in a bad mood*** 心情不好

score〔skor〕*n.* 分數　　***after all*** 畢竟

grade〔gred〕*n.* 成績　　***the end of the world*** 世界末日

see A as B 視 A 為 B　　***do better*** 考得更好

relax〔rɪˈlæks〕*v.* 放輕鬆　　***forget about*** 忘記

stress〔strɛs〕*n.* 壓力（*= pressure*）

How about…? …如何？（*= What about…?*）

go for a bike ride 去騎腳踏車　　beach〔bitʃ〕*n.* 海邊

along the way 一路上；沿途　　***take a picture*** 拍照

stretch〔strɛtʃ〕*v.* 伸展　　guarantee〔͵gærənˈti〕*v.* 保證

afterward〔ˈæftəwəd〕*adv.* 之後

68. **Hang in There**

Dear Donald,

I haven't seen you since you moved away from our neighborhood. *Last week*, I saw a message posted on your Facebook page that your father was injured at work. I know this must be a financial burden on your family. I really wish I could help you in some way.

Difficult as the financial problems are, you still have to stand up to the test of it and never give in or give up. Perhaps working part-time could help you make both ends meet. *Also*, you can borrow money from me if you have any difficulties. Just keep in mind that everything will be fine eventually and always be optimistic. *There is a light at the end of the tunnel.*

I hope your father has a speedy recovery and I hope to hear from you soon! *Don't hesitate to call if there is anything you need.*

Your devoted friend,

Nelson

68. 要堅持下去

親愛的唐納德：

　　自從你搬離我們這個社區之後，我就很久沒見到你了。上星期，我看到你在臉書上發布你父親在工作時受傷的訊息。我知道這對你們家一定會造成經濟上的負擔，我真希望能幫上你的忙。

　　雖然財務問題很困難，但你還是要經得起這次的考驗，絕不要屈服或放棄。也許打工能幫助你收支平衡。儘管如此，如果你有任何困難，可以向我借錢。只要記得，一切到最後都會好轉，而且一定要保持樂觀，就快要柳暗花明了。

　　我希望你的父親能早日康復，我也希望能很快就收到你的信！如果有任何需要，儘管打電話給我。

你誠摯的朋友，
尼爾森

＊＊　————————————

hang in there 堅持下去
neighborhood〔'nebəˌhʊd〕*n.* 鄰近地區
post〔post〕*v.*（在網路上）張貼訊息　　injure〔'ɪndʒə〕*v.* 傷害
at work 工作中；在工作場所　　financial〔fə'nænʃəl〕*adj.* 財務的
burden〔'bɝdn̩〕*n.* 負擔　　***in some way*** 以某種方式
Difficult *as* the financial problems are, ... 雖然財務問題很困難，…
　　(= *Though the financial problems are difficult,...*)
stand up to 抵禦；對抗；經得起　　test〔tɛst〕*n.* 考驗
give in 屈服　　***give up*** 放棄　　***work part-time*** 打工
make both ends meet 使收支平衡；量入為出
keep in mind 把…牢記在心　　go〔go〕*v.* 進展
eventually〔ɪ'vɛntʃʊəlɪ〕*adv.* 最後
optimistic〔ˌɑptə'mɪstɪk〕*adj.* 樂觀的　　tunnel〔'tʌnl̩〕*n.* 隧道
light at the end of the tunnel 光明在望；柳暗花明
speedy〔'spidɪ〕*adj.* 迅速的　　recovery〔rɪ'kʌvərɪ〕*n.* 康復
hear from 收到…的信　　hesitate〔'hɛzəˌtet〕*v.* 猶豫

69. One Door Closes, Another Opens

Dear Emma,

I know that you really wanted to study medicine at NTU. I also know how hard you worked to achieve your dream. The competition is intense. You really have to be the best of the best to enter NTU. *However,* sometimes life doesn't work out the way we want or expect. That's just the way it goes.

Remember the saying: When one door closes, another opens. *Just because you failed this time doesn't mean you should give up.* There's still time for you to improve your grades, Emma. You can take the test again in three months. You should seize every opportunity to study. Maybe you can't study medicine at NTU. That doesn't mean you can't study it somewhere else. Perhaps your dream hasn't vanished after all.

The main point is: don't give up. Think of this as a chance to re-evaluate what you want to do. I have faith in you! Just stay positive.

Sincerely,

David

69. 當一扇門關上時，另一扇門會開啟

親愛的艾瑪：

　　我知道妳很想唸台灣大學醫學系，我也知道妳努力想要達成妳的夢想。競爭很激烈，妳必須是菁英中的菁英才能進入國立台灣大學。但是有些時候，生命並不會如我們所預期。這就是萬物的法則。

　　記住這句話：「當一扇門關上時，另一扇門會開啟。」只因為妳這次失敗，並不代表妳應該放棄。艾瑪，改善妳的成績還是來得及的。三個月後妳可以再考一次，妳應該要把握住每個唸書的機會，或許妳不能唸台大醫學系，但那不表示妳不能唸別間學校的醫學系。或許妳的夢想終究還未破滅。

　　重點是，不要放棄。就把這當作是一次重新評估妳目標的機會。我對妳有信心。一定要保持積極進取的精神。

大衛　敬上

**

medicine〔'mɛdəsn̩〕*n.* 醫學
NTU 國立台灣大學（= *National Taiwan University*）
achieve〔ə'tʃiv〕*v.* 達成　　competition〔,kɑmpə'tɪʃən〕*n.* 競爭
intense〔ɪn'tɛns〕*adj.* 激烈的
the best of the best 菁英中的菁英　　***work out*** 發展
expect〔ɪk'spɛkt〕*v.* 期待　　go〔go〕*v.* 進展
give up 放棄　　improve〔ɪm'pruv〕*v.* 改善
seize〔siz〕*v.* 抓住　　opportunity〔,ɑpə'tjunətɪ〕*n.* 機會
after all 畢竟；終究　　point〔pɔɪnt〕*n.* 重點
re-evaluate〔,rɪɪ'væljʊ,et〕*v.* 重新評估　　faith〔feθ〕*n.* 信心
positive〔'pɑzətɪv〕*adj.* 正面的；積極的；樂觀的

70. A Show of Respect

Dear Ken,

How are you these days? We have just finished the challenge of our lives. Soon, we will graduate from school and become college students. I'm so surprised that the time passed so fast!

I just wanted to tell you a few things. *First*, you were the best class leader I ever knew. *We all had deep respect for you*. *Also*, you were the best chess club leader of all-time. You always tackled things passionately. *I admired your tenacity*. All of our classmates consider ourselves fortunate to have known you. We had the most wonderful time in the club. You're a great chess player and I often envy your talent. You won many awards, but I won nothing. *However*, you never had contempt for me. *Instead*, you tried to help me. I will never forget your kindness. That's why so many people are willing to be your friend.

I hope that after we graduate, *we can stay in touch*. Maybe we can still play chess together. It would be great to talk about our memories of high school life.

Best wishes,

Jill

70. 表示敬意

親愛的肯：

　　你最近好嗎？我們才剛結束我們人生中的挑戰。很快的，我們將從學校畢業，成爲大學生。我很驚訝時間過得這麼快！

　　我只是要告訴你一些事情。首先，你是我所見過最棒的班長，我們都深深地尊敬你。而且你也是歷年來最棒的西洋棋社的社長，你處理事情總是充滿熱情，我很欽佩你的毅力。所有的同學都覺得自己很幸運，可以認識你。我們在社團裡渡過美好的時光，你是最好的西洋棋手，而我也常常羨慕你的天份。你得過許多獎，而我卻一個都沒有。然而，你從不輕視我，反而很努力想幫助我。我永遠都不會忘記你的好心，那就是爲什麼有這麼多人都願意當你的朋友的原因。

　　希望畢業之後，我們可以保持聯絡。或許我們仍可以一起下西洋棋，能夠談談高中生活的回憶，將會是很棒的一件事。

寄上最誠摯的祝福，
吉兒

＊＊ ────────────

challenge〔'tʃælɪndʒ〕*n.* 挑戰　　chess〔tʃɛs〕*n.* 西洋棋
club leader 社長　　***of all-time*** 空前的；史無前例的
tackle〔'tækl̩〕*v.* 處理　　passionately〔'pæʃənɪtlɪ〕*adv.* 熱情地
admire〔əd'maɪr〕*v.* 讚賞；欽佩
tenacity〔tɪ'næsətɪ〕*n.* 毅力；不屈不撓　　envy〔'ɛnvɪ〕*v.* 羨慕
award〔ə'wɔrd〕*n.* 獎　　contempt〔kən'tɛmpt〕*n.* 輕視
have contempt for *sb.* 輕視某人（ = *hold sb. in contempt*）
instead〔ɪn'stɛd〕*adv.* 取而代之；反而
willing〔'wɪlɪŋ〕*adj.* 願意的　　***stay in touch*** 保持聯絡
memory〔'mɛmərɪ〕*n.* 記憶

71. A Letter to an Idol

Dear Lady Gaga,

I have admired your talent for a long time. The first time I saw you sparkling on the stage, I thought, "What a unique singer!" You looked so different from anyone I had seen before. That impression has remained in my mind since then.

In the following years, you grew more and more popular. I kept following you, and I found that your music is amazing! Not only that, but the way you dress is always surprising. You always follow your own style and never care what others think. *I just had to write to you and tell you how much I appreciate you.* Please, continue to be yourself and keep your style forever! If you do, I will always be your fan.

Sincerely yours,
Charles

71. 給偶像的一封信

親愛的女神卡卡：

　　我欽佩妳的才華好一段時間了，第一次看到妳在舞台上發光發熱時，我心裡想：「好特別的一個明星啊！」妳看起來跟我之前看到的人有很大的不同，從那時起，妳就在我心中留下難以抹滅的印象。

　　接下來的幾年，妳的人氣扶搖直上。我一直都密切注意著妳，我覺得妳的音樂好棒！不僅如此，妳穿搭衣服的方式也總是充滿驚喜。妳總是走自己的風格，不在乎其他人的眼光。我只是想寫信跟妳說我有多麼欣賞妳。請繼續做妳自己，永遠保有自己的風格！如果妳能這樣，我永遠都會是妳的歌迷。

查爾斯　敬上

** ────────────────

admire〔əd'maɪr〕v. 讚賞　　talent〔'tælənt〕n. 才能
sparkle〔'spɑrkḷ〕v. 閃耀；閃亮　　stage〔stedʒ〕n. 舞台
unique〔ju'nik〕adj. 獨特的
impression〔ɪm'prɛʃən〕n. 印象
remain〔rɪ'men〕v. 仍然
following〔'faloɪŋ〕adj. 接下來的　　grow〔gro〕v. 變得
follow〔'falo〕v. 密切注意；順從
care〔kɛr〕v. 在意　　amazing〔ə'mezɪŋ〕adj. 驚人的
not only…**but (also)** 不僅…而且　　dress〔drɛs〕v. 穿衣服
appreciate〔ə'priʃɪ,et〕v. 欣賞
forever〔fə'ɛvə〕adv. 永遠　　fan〔fæn〕n. 迷

72. A Letter to the Editor

Dear Editor,

My name is Joe. I like to travel, and I've been to a lot of different countries. Last month, I visited Taiwan for ten days. I think it was one of the most impressive experiences that I've ever had.

At first, I thought Taiwan was just a small island without appealing scenery. *However*, after traveling around it, I have totally changed my thinking. The rich variety of animals, the fresh air of the countryside, and the hospitable people all amazed me. I still remember one night in particular. I had taken a stroll along the beach. The sea wind blowing my hair was so comfortable and the place was so quiet. I raised my head to look at the sky. The stars and the moon were so beautiful that I couldn't take my eyes off them. *That scene has been etched into my mind.*

Now I'm back home, but I can't forget the things I saw in Taiwan. If I can, I'll visit there again!

Sincerely yours,

Joe

72. 給編輯的一封信

親愛的編輯：

　　我叫作喬，我喜歡旅行，我去過很多不同的國家。上個月，我來訪台灣十天，我想這是我這一生中最印象深刻的體驗之一。

　　一開始，我以爲台灣只是個沒有漂亮風景的小島。但是，遊歷過後，我完全改變了我的想法。種類豐富的動物、鄉間的新鮮空氣，以及好客的民眾，全都令我驚訝。我還記得有個特別的夜晚。我在海灘漫步，輕撫過我頭髮的海風相當舒服，四周也很寧靜，我抬頭仰望天空，星星跟月亮美到我捨不得把視線移開，那景象深深地烙印在我的腦海裡。

　　現在我回到家，仍舊無法忘懷在台灣看到的一切。如果可以的話，我會再次造訪台灣！

喬　　敬上

** ─────────────

editor〔ˈɛdɪtə〕*n.* 編輯
impressive〔ɪmˈprɛsɪv〕*adj.* 令人印象深刻的
appealing〔əˈpilɪŋ〕*adj.* 吸引人的
scenery〔ˈsinərɪ〕*n.* 風景
variety〔vəˈraɪətɪ〕*n.* 種類；多樣性
fresh〔frɛʃ〕*adj.* 新鮮的
countryside〔ˈkʌntrɪˌsaɪd〕*n.* 鄉下
hospitable〔ˈhɑspɪtəbḷ〕*adj.* 好客的
amaze〔əˈmez〕*v.* 使驚奇　　***in particular*** 尤其
take a stroll 散步　　　raise〔rez〕*v.* 舉起；抬起
take *one's **eyes off*** 將目光從…上面移開
scene〔sin〕*n.* 情景
etch〔ɛtʃ〕*v.* 鮮明地刻劃；將…深印（於心裡）

73. A Complaint Letter

Dear Sales Manager,

I am writing to you concerning a dress (product #053821) that I bought from your company recently. The dress that was delivered is totally different from the picture I saw on your website. The sleeves are much longer than shown and the length is much shorter. Instead of having buttons down the back, the dress has buttons in the front. But most important of all, the color is bright green, not the beautiful amber I wanted. I would like to have a new dress that looks the same as the one pictured on your website.

In addition, I think your company must be responsible for all shipping fees, and should send the new dress to me express delivery. *It is intended as a birthday present for my sister and must arrive within three days.* Should the dress be out of stock, I expect to receive a full refund, including the shipping charges. In the meantime, I have contacted my bank and placed a stop payment order on the credit card charge. I will not agree to pay for the dress until I am satisfied. *I look forward to your prompt reply.*

Sincerely,

Jill Smith

73. 一封抱怨信

親愛的銷售經理：

　　我寫這封信，是要談論有關我最近從貴公司購買的一件洋裝（產品編號：053821）。我收到的洋裝跟我在你們的網站上看到的圖片完全不一樣。袖子比網站上看到的長很多，而長度則比較短。衣服後面底下沒有鈕扣，前面反而有。而且最重要的是，顏色是鮮綠色的，而不是我想要的漂亮琥珀色。我想要一件跟網站圖片上一模一樣的新洋裝。

　　此外，我認為貴公司必須負擔所有的運費，而且要將新洋裝以快遞的方式寄給我。這是我打算送給我姐姐的生日禮物，所以必須在三天內送達。萬一洋裝沒有庫存，我希望能全額退費，包括運費。同時，我已連絡我的銀行，停止信用卡付款。除非我滿意，否則我不會同意支付這件洋裝的費用。我期待你們能盡快回覆。

　　　　　　　　　　　　　　　　吉兒史密斯 敬上

**　————————————

concerning〔kən'sɜnɪŋ〕*prep.* 關於（= *about*）
website〔'wɛb,saɪt〕*n.* 網站　　sleeve〔sliv〕*n.* 袖子
instead of 不…而　　button〔'bʌtn̩〕*n.* 扣子
most important of all 最重要的是
amber〔'æmbɚ〕*n.* 琥珀色　　picture〔'pɪktʃɚ〕*v.* 拍攝
in addition 此外　　*be responsible for* 負責…
shipping fee 運費　　express〔ɪk'sprɛs〕*adj.* 快遞的
express delivery 使用快遞服務　　intend〔ɪn'tɛnd〕*v.* 打算
should〔ʃʊd〕*aux.* 萬一　　*out of stock* 無庫存
refund〔'ri,fʌnd〕*n.* 退款　　charge〔tʃɑrdʒ〕*n.* 費用
in the meantime 同時　　contact〔'kɑntækt〕*v.* 聯絡
place an order 下命令；下訂單　　*look forward to* 期待
prompt〔prɑmpt〕*adj.* 迅速的；立即的

74. A Letter of Complaint

Dear Sir,

Your bakery is the most famous one in the area near my home. *However,* I recently had a terrible experience with your store. Last week, I walked into to your bakery to order an eight-inch strawberry cake because I wanted to celebrate my best friend's birthday. But the clerk was inattentive and didn't hear what I said at all. This was the first unhappy experience.

What made me even angrier was that when I got the cake I ordered and opened it, I found out that it was a six-inch chocolate cake. *Fortunately,* my friend also likes chocolate. But this wasn't the most terrible part. When we cut the cake, we were shocked to see many giant ants climbing out of it. My friend was so terrified that she jumped out of the chair. I kept saying sorry to her and we both lost our appetite. *In short,* I was completely disappointed by your service. It was the most disgusting birthday cake I have ever had. *I must insist that you give back my money and apologize, or I will never shop in your bakery again!*

Your customer,

Joe Smith

74. 一封抱怨信

先生你好：

　　你們的麵包店是我家附近最有名的，但是最近我在你們店裡有一次很糟糕的經驗。上星期因爲我要替我最好的朋友慶生，所以我去你們店裡訂購了一個八吋的草莓蛋糕，但是店員心不在焉的，而且根本沒有在聽我說的話，這是第一次不愉快的經驗。

　　讓我更生氣的是，當我拿到蛋糕，打開來看的時候，我發現是六吋的巧克力蛋糕。幸好，我的朋友也喜歡巧克力，但是，這都還不是最糟的部分。當我們切開蛋糕的時候，很多大螞蟻從裡頭爬了出來，嚇了我們一跳。我朋友還嚇到從椅子上跳起來。我一直跟她道歉，我們後來都沒胃口了。簡單來說，我對你們的服務很失望，那是我看過最噁心的生日蛋糕。我必須堅持你們要退費，並道歉，否則我就再也不會去你們店裡消費了！

顧客
喬・史密斯

---

complaint〔kəmˈplent〕 *n.* 抱怨
bakery〔ˈbekərɪ〕 *n.* 麵包店
celebrate〔ˈsɛləˌbret〕 *v.* 慶祝　　clerk〔klɝk〕 *n.* 店員
inattentive〔ˌɪnəˈtɛntɪv〕 *adj.* 不注意的
fortunately〔ˈfɔrtʃənɪtlɪ〕 *adv.* 幸運地
shocked〔ʃɑkt〕 *adj.* 震驚的　　giant〔ˈdʒaɪənt〕 *adj.* 巨大的
ant〔ænt〕 *n.* 螞蟻　　appetite〔ˈæpəˌtaɪt〕 *n.* 胃口
in short 簡言之　　disgusting〔dɪsˈɡʌstɪŋ〕 *adj.* 噁心的
insist〔ɪnˈsɪst〕 *v.* 堅持
apologize〔əˈpɑləˌdʒaɪz〕 *v.* 道歉

75. A Letter to the Mayor

Dear Mr. Mayor,

I have played golf for many years, and I really enjoy playing golf at the golf range near my house. I play it every Sunday. Though I love the golf range, I am not happy about the disregard for the rules there. I sometimes see some people smoking on the range where it is not allowed. *Not only is this harmful to nonsmokers, but it is against the law.*

As you know, smoking is banned in certain public areas. I complained to the staff and manager of the golf range several times, but nothing was done. *Then* I lodged a formal complaint with the Health Department, which is in charge of enforcing the anti-smoking regulations. *Again,* there was no result.

Now I am appealing to you. I hope that you will contact the persons in charge of enforcing this regulation and direct them to take action. Thank you.

Cordially,

Beth Lee

75. 給市長的一封信

親愛的市長先生：

　　我打高爾夫球打了很多年，我真的很喜歡在我家附近的高爾夫球練習場打球。我每個星期天都打高爾夫球。雖然我很喜歡那座高爾夫球練習場，但卻不滿意那裡忽視政府的規定。有時我會看到一些人在高爾夫球練習場抽煙，而那是不被允許的。不僅對不抽煙的人有害，也違反法律。

　　正如您所知，在某些公共區域是禁止吸煙的。我向那裡的員工和經理投訴好幾次，但他們卻什麼也沒做。然後我就向負責執行禁煙規定的衛生部提出正式的投訴，同樣也沒有結果。

　　現在我要懇求您，我希望您能聯絡負責執行這項規定的人，並指示他們要採取行動。謝謝您。

李貝絲　敬上

**

mayor (ˋmeɚ) *n.* 市長　　***play golf*** 打高爾夫球

range (rendʒ) *n.* 高爾夫球練習場

disregard (͵dɪsrɪˋgɑrd) *n.* 忽視

not only…but (also) 不僅…而且

nonsmoker (ˋnɑnˋsmokɚ) *n.* 不抽煙的人

against (əˋgɛnst) *prep.* 違反　　ban (bæn) *v.* 禁止

certain (ˋsɝtn̩) *adj.* 某些　　complain (kəmˋplen) *v.* 抱怨；投訴

staff (stæf) *n.* 員工　　lodge (lɑdʒ) *v.* 正式提出

complaint (kəmˋplent) *n.* 抱怨；申訴

the Health Department 衛生部　　***in charge of*** 負責

enforce (ɪnˋfors) *v.* 執行　　anti-smoking *adj.* 禁止吸煙的

regulation (͵rɛgjəˋleʃən) *n.* 規定　　***appeal to*** 請求；呼籲

contact (ˋkɑntækt) *v.* 連絡　　direct (dəˋrɛkt) *v.* 指示；命令

take action 採取行動　　cordially (ˋkɔrdʒəlɪ) *adv.* 衷心地；誠摯地

76. A Letter to the Editor

Dear Editor,

Yesterday, your newspaper published an article about our school. *However*, I would like to tell you that you were definitely misinformed. The report said that our principal was spotted taking bribes from a construction company on May 5th. You had no evidence to back up the allegations; *instead*, you acted irresponsibly by spreading rumors.

I can swear that our principal is innocent because May 5th was the day of our school festival, and I served and helped our principal. We were busy helping other students to decorate the school, so the principal had no chance to meet with the construction company. There is no way he could have slipped away to accept a bribe.

I strongly demand a retraction and an apology as soon as possible. It is your responsibility to publish the truth. I'm sure that you are wise enough to do the right thing and save the reputation of our school and our principal.

Sincerely,

Helen Lee

76. 給編輯的一封信

親愛的編輯：

　　昨天你們的報紙刊登了一篇關於我們學校的文章，但是我想告訴你們，消息的來源是錯誤的。那篇報導說，有人目擊我們的校長在五月五號收受建商的賄款，你們並沒有證據支持那項指控，反而不負責任地散播謠言。

　　我發誓我們的校長是清白的，因為五月五號是我們學校的校慶，而我在校長旁邊幫忙。我們忙著幫助其他學生佈置學校，所以校長根本沒機會跟建商見面，他不可能溜走去收取賄款。

　　我強烈要求你們儘快把話收回並且道歉。你們必須負責刊登事實。我相信你們很聰明，會做正確的事，並挽救我們學校以及校長的名聲。

李海倫　敬上

**

publish〔ˋpʌblɪʃ〕v. 刊登　　article〔ˋɑrtɪkḷ〕n. 文章
definitely〔ˋdɛfənɪtlɪ〕adv. 一定
misinform〔͵mɪsɪnˋfɔrm〕v. 給…錯誤消息
principal〔ˋprɪnsəpḷ〕n. 校長　　spot〔spɑt〕v. 看見
bribe〔ˋbraɪb〕n. 賄賂　　construction〔kənˋstrʌkʃən〕n. 建造
evidence〔ˋɛvədəns〕n. 證據　　***back up*** 支持
allegation〔͵æləˋgeʃən〕n. 指控　　act〔ækt〕v. 表現
irresponsibly〔͵ɪrɪˋspɑnsəblɪ〕adv. 不負責任地
spread〔ˋsprɛd〕v. 散佈　　rumor〔ˋrumɚ〕n. 謠言
innocent〔ˋɪnəsn̩t〕adj. 清白的；無辜的
decorate〔ˋdɛkə͵ret〕v. 裝飾　　slip〔ˋslɪp〕v. 溜走
demand〔dʊˋmænd〕v. 要求
retraction〔rɪˋtrækʃən〕n.（說過的話）收回
apology〔əˋpɑlədʒɪ〕n. 道歉　　reputation〔͵rɛpjəˋteʃən〕n. 名聲

77. **Surgery Gone Bad**

Dear Doctor,

You performed surgery on me last Saturday. The surgery was supposed to change my appearance. I had hoped you would make me look more handsome. That is what you promised. *However*, something went very wrong. My face is a disaster. It is full of wrinkles and creases. There are itchy red patches all over my cheeks. My friends say I look like an old man.

This has caused me a great deal of pain. I cannot even leave the house. I do not want others to see my ugly face. *Moreover*, the pain has caused me to become depressed.

Here is what I want from you. As soon as possible, I want you to correct the mistakes you made. You promised to enhance my appearance. You owe that to me. This correction will also be done free of charge. *If you do not cooperate, I will be forced to consult an attorney*.

Sincerely,

Jack Lee

77. 失敗的手術

親愛的醫生：

　　上星期你替我動了手術。手術本來應該可以改變我的外表，我原本希望你能把我變得更帥一點，那是你承諾過我的。但是，手術出了很大的差錯，我的臉整個毀了，充滿了皺紋跟皺褶。我的臉頰上佈滿了發癢難耐的紅斑。我朋友都說我看起來像一個老人。

　　這件事造成我很大的痛苦，我甚至無法出門，我不想讓其他人看到我醜陋的臉。而且，這痛苦也讓我變得非常沮喪。

　　以下就是我對你的要求。我希望你能儘快把你在我臉上所犯的錯修正回來。你承諾過你會讓我的外表更好，這是你欠我的。這次的修正也得是免費的。如果你不肯合作，我就不得不去找律師了。

傑克　敬上

** ————————————————————

surgery〔ˈsɝdʒərɪ〕n. 手術　　***go bad*** 出差錯
perform〔pɚˈfɔrm〕v. 執行　　***be supposed to*** 應該
appearance〔əˈpɪrəns〕n. 外表
handsome〔ˈhænsəm〕adj. 英俊的
promise〔ˈprɑmɪs〕v. 答應　　disaster〔dɪzˈæstɚ〕n. 災難
be full of 充滿了　　wrinkle〔ˈrɪŋkḷ〕n. 皺紋
crease〔kris〕n. 皺褶　　itchy〔ˈɪtʃɪ〕adj. 發癢的
patch〔pætʃ〕n. 斑點　　cheek〔tʃik〕n. 臉頰
ugly〔ˈʌglɪ〕adj. 醜的　　cause〔kɔz〕v. 使
depressed〔dɪˈprɛst〕adj. 沮喪的　　correct〔kəˈrɛkt〕v. 更正
enhance〔ɪnˈhæns〕v. 增進　　owe〔o〕v. 欠
free of charge 免費地　　cooperate〔koˈɑpəˌret〕v. 合作
force〔fors〕v. 強迫；使不得不　　consult〔kənˈsʌlt〕v. 請教
attorney〔əˈtɝnɪ〕n. 律師 (= *lawyer*)

78. A Bad Trip

To Whom It May Concern:

Last week, I joined your tour to Thailand. *However*, I am furious about certain events that took place.

First, at the airport, the tour guide didn't appear in time to help us check in for our flight. *Second*, the first night in Bangkok, our hotel didn't have our reservation. *Then*, the hotel in which we stayed was the most disgusting hotel I have ever seen! The mirror in the bathroom was broken and the sheets smelled like rotten eggs. *What's worse*, the door would not lock!

For a worldwide famous travel company, your poor service is shocking. Everything on this tour was a tragedy. I am almost embarrassed to tell my family about it. *You should treat your customers better*, *or your company won't be prosperous anymore!*

Sincerely,
Jack Lee

78. 一趟糟糕的旅行

敬啓者：

　　上星期我參加了你們到泰國的行程，但是我對某些發生的事情感到非常憤怒。

　　首先，在機場的時候，導遊並沒有及時出現，幫我們辦理登機。第二，在曼谷的第一天晚上，飯店沒有我們的訂房資料。然後，我們住的飯店眞的是我看過最噁心的飯店！浴室的鏡子破裂，而且床單聞起來像臭掉的雞蛋。更糟的是，門鎖不起來！

　　對於一個世界知名的旅遊公司來說，你們差勁的服務眞令人震驚。這趟旅行的一切都是悲劇。跟我家人談到這個旅程時，眞令我尷尬。你們應該更善待顧客，否則你們公司的生意不可能再這麼好了！

李傑克　敬上

** ──────────

tour〔tʊr〕*n.* 旅行　　Thailand〔'taɪlənd〕*n.* 泰國
furious〔'fjurɪəs〕*adj.* 狂怒的　　certain〔'sɝtn̩〕*adv.* 某些
event〔ɪ'vɛnt〕*n.* 事件　　***take place*** 發生
airport〔'ɛr,port〕*n.* 機場　　***tour guide*** 導遊
appear〔ə'pɪr〕*v.* 出現　　***in time*** 及時
check in 辦理登機手續　　flight〔flaɪt〕*n.* 班機
Bangkok〔'bæŋkɑk〕*n.* 曼谷【泰國首都】
reservation〔,rɛzə'veʃən〕*n.* 預訂　　stay〔ste〕*v.* 暫住
disgusting〔dɪs'gʌstɪŋ〕*adj.* 噁心的　　mirror〔'mɪrɚ〕*n.* 鏡子
sheets〔ʃits〕*n. pl.* 床單　　rotten〔'rɑtn̩〕*adj.* 腐壞的
what's worse 更糟的是　　lock〔lɑk〕*v.* 上鎖
worldwide〔'wɝld'waɪd〕*adv.* 在全世界
shocking〔'ʃɑkɪŋ〕*adj.* 令人震驚的　　tragedy〔'trædʒədɪ〕*n.* 悲劇
treat〔trit〕*v.* 對待　　prosperous〔'prɑspərəs〕*adj.* 繁榮的；成功的
not…anymore 不再…

79. A Letter Asking for Independence

Dear Mom,

It seems that we have often been at odds recently, and we have even had some unpleasant arguments. I don't want to complain about this or try to excuse myself. *Instead*, I hope to explain my feelings so that we can better understand one another.

First, I want to tell you how truly grateful I am for your selfless devotion. You have spared no effort in looking after me. *You always want me to do the right thing and make the right decisions*. It is true that children are too young to decide many things on their own. *However*, overprotection can frustrate them. Lately, it seems like everything I do is irrational and inappropriate in your eyes.

I am eighteen years old now, and this is a good age for me to start making my own decisions. *One day*, I will have to take care of myself and be responsible for my behavior. It makes sense to me that I should start practicing now, while I still have the benefit of your guidance. I am looking forward to your understanding. *I am sure that if we just put ourselves in one another's shoes, we can live in harmony*.

Sincerely,

Phil

79. 一封要求獨立的信

親愛的媽媽：

　　我們似乎最近處得不是很好，甚至還起了一些不愉快的爭執。我不是想要抱怨或是為自己找藉口。相反地，我想說出我的感受，這樣我們才能更了解彼此。

　　首先，我想告訴您，我有多感激您無私的奉獻。您一直不遺餘力地照顧我。您總是要我做對的事以及做出正確的決定。的確，小孩子年紀太小，無法自己決定很多事。但是，過度保護也會使他們感到挫折。最近，似乎在您眼中，我所做的每件事，都不理性而且不恰當。

　　我現在已經十八歲了，對我來說，也是我該開始自己做決定的年齡了。將來有一天，我也得照顧自己，並為自己的行為負責。我現在開始練習獨立也是合理的，同時還可以受惠於您的指導。我期待您的諒解。我確信如果我們彼此能設身處地為對方著想，我們就可以和諧相處。

菲爾　敬上

＊＊ ────────────────

at odds 爭吵；不和　　recently〔ˈrisn̩tlɪ〕 *adv.* 最近

argument〔ˈɑrgjəmənt〕 *n.* 爭論

excuse〔ɪkˈskjuz〕 *v.* 替…找藉口

grateful〔ˈgretfəl〕 *adj.* 感激的　　selfless〔ˈsɛlflɪs〕 *adj.* 無私的

devotion〔dɪˈvoʃən〕 *n.* 奉獻　　*spare no effort* 不遺餘力

look after 照顧　　frustrate〔ˈfrʌstret〕 *v.* 使受挫

irrational〔ɪˈræʃənl̩〕 *adj.* 不理性的

inappropriate〔ˌɪnəˈproprɪɪt〕 *adj.* 不適當的

make sense 合理　　benefit〔ˈbɛnəfɪt〕 *n.* 利益；好處

guidance〔ˈgaɪdn̩s〕 *n.* 指導　　*look forward to* 期待

put oneself in sb's shoes 站在別人的立場想

harmony〔ˈhɑrmənɪ〕 *n.* 和諧

80. Being Open with a Parent

Dear Dad,

I know you and Mom have quarreled recently. She regards you as a lazy husband who never pitches in around the house. *Meanwhile*, you dismiss her as an inconsiderate wife who assigns you a lot of troublesome work after you get home from work.

As far as I am concerned, you are more to blame than Mom is. Although you may be exhausted after a day of work, it isn't a proper excuse to evade such chores. You always tell me to be a responsible man, and I think you should demonstrate it first. If you are extremely tired when you get home, you can ask me to do your housework instead of complaining all night. I expect you and Mom to get along well with each other. I want to live in a harmonious family.

By the way, I think you owe Mom an apology. Fortunately, I got two movie tickets from my friends a couple days ago. You can go on a date with Mom this weekend. Take her to the movies and show how much you love her. *Last but not least*, don't forget to apologize for your poor behavior. I hope to see you change.

Best wishes,

Peter

80.　對父（母）開誠佈公

親愛的爸爸：

　　我知道你跟媽媽最近在吵架。她認為你是個懶惰的丈夫，從不幫忙做家事。另一方面，你認為她是不體貼的妻子，在你下班後，還分派許多麻煩的工作給你。

　　就我而言，你比媽媽還該受責備。雖然上了一天班後，你可能很累，但這不是逃避家事的適當藉口。你總是告訴我要當一個負責任的男人，我認為你應該先以身作則。如果你回到家真的很累，你可以要求我替你做家事，而不是整晚抱怨。我期待你跟媽媽能好好相處。我想要有和諧的家庭生活。

　　順便一提，我覺得你欠媽媽一個道歉。很幸運地，我幾天前從朋友那裡拿到了兩張電影票，這個週末你可以和媽媽一起去約會。帶她去看電影，表現出你有多愛她。最後一項要點是，別忘了要為你不良的行為道歉。希望可以看到你的改變。

寄上最誠摯的祝福，
彼得

**

open〔'opən〕*adj.* 坦白的　　quarrel〔'kwɔrəl〕*v.* 吵架
regard A *as* B 認為 A 是 B　　*pitch in* 努力做事；有貢獻
meanwhile〔'min,hwaɪl〕*adv.* 另一方面
dismiss〔dɪs'mɪs〕*v.* 摒棄；對…不屑一提
inconsiderate〔,ɪnkən'sɪdərɪt〕*adj.* 不體貼的
assign〔ə'saɪn〕*v.* 分配；分派
as far as sb. *be concerned* 就某人而言　　*be to blame* 該受責備
exhausted〔ɪg'zɔstɪd〕*adj.* 筋疲力盡的　　evade〔ɪ'ved〕*v.* 逃避
cover〔'kʌvɚ〕*v.* 處理；代替（某人）　　*get along* 相處
harmonious〔har:monɪəs〕*adj.* 和諧的　　*by the way* 順便一提
owe〔o〕*v.* 欠　　apology〔ə'pɑlədʒɪ〕*n.* 道歉
go on a date 去約會　　*last but not least* 最後一項要點是

81. Asking for Cooperation from a Neighbor

Dear Ken,

Hello, neighbor. Welcome to our building. Everyone is very friendly here. *We like to keep the lines of communication open.* I'm writing to discuss a situation that affects us both.

It appears that you are remodeling your apartment. I'm aware of this because I can hear the construction noise. You see, I am a third-year high school student. That means I am studying for the college entrance exam. This is obviously an important time for me. *I have tons of homework and I am very stressed out.* The problem is the noise. I am not able to concentrate on my studies. It wouldn't be so bad if you worked during the day. I am at school during these hours. The issue is the noise at night.

I'm hoping we can come to some sort of agreement. All I am asking is that you limit the noise during the evening hours. I would appreciate it very much. *Feel free to contact me at any time to discuss this matter.* Thanks for your cooperation.

Sincerely,

Jill Lee

81. 尋求鄰居的合作

親愛的肯：

　　哈囉，我的鄰居，歡迎來到我們的大廈。這裡的人都很友善，我們喜歡保持溝通管道的暢通。我寫信的目的是想討論一個影響到我們雙方的情況。

　　看起來你正在重新整修你的公寓，我會知道是因為我有聽到施工的噪音。你知道的，我是個高三學生，所以我正在準備大學入學考試。這段期間對我來說顯然很重要，我有很多作業，而且我的壓力很大。問題就是噪音，我無法專注在課業上。如果你們是白天施工，情況可能不會這麼糟，因為這段時間我在學校。

　　我希望我們能達成共識，我要要求的，就是晚上你能控制一下噪音，我會很感激。隨時都可以來找我討論這件事，謝謝你的合作。

　　　　　　　　　　　　　　　　　　　　　李吉兒　　敬上

**

communication〔kə͵mjunə'keʃən〕n. 溝通
communication lines 溝通管道
situation〔͵sɪtʃʊ'eʃən〕n. 情況　　affect〔ə'fɛkt〕v. 影響
appear〔ə'pɪr〕v. 似乎　　remodel〔ri'mɑdl〕v. 重新整修
apartment〔ə'partmənt〕n. 公寓　　aware〔ə'wɛr〕adj. 知道的
construction〔kən'strʌkʃən〕n. 建造
college entrance exam 大學入學考試
obviously〔'ɑbvɪəslɪ〕adv. 明顯地　　***tons of*** 很多
stressed out 有壓力的；緊張的　　***concentrate on*** 專心於
studies〔'stʌdɪz〕n. pl. 學業　　hours〔aʊrz〕n. pl. 時間
issue〔'ɪʃu〕n. 問題　　agreement〔ə'grimənt〕n. 協議
come to some sort of agreement 達成某種協議
appreciate〔ə'priʃɪ͵et〕v. 感激　　contact〔'kɑntækt〕v. 聯絡
matter〔'mætɚ〕n. 事情　　cooperation〔ko͵apə'reʃən〕n. 合作

82. Living on Campus

Dear Mom and Dad,

I know you want me to live at home while I attend university, but I would prefer to live on campus for several reasons. *First*, I'm not a child. After I graduate from high school, I will legally be an adult. *Second*, I must learn to be independent. I can't continue to depend on you for everything. If I do, I won't be able to compete with other people in the future. *Also*, there is very little risk for me to live on campus. *After all*, it will be full of people just like me.

Please forgive me for what I'm about to say. I know it is hard for you to let me go, but it is my life. *I want to meet more challenges and learn how to overcome them.* Please let me go!

Love,
Jack

82. 住 校

親愛的爸媽：

　　我知道我上大學後你們想要我住在家裡，但是因為幾個理由，我想要住在學校。首先，我已經不是小孩了，高中畢業後，法律上來說，我就已經是個成人了。第二，我必須學會獨立，我不能再靠你們來提供我一切。如果我繼續依賴你們，在未來，我就無法跟其他人競爭。此外，住在學校對我來說也沒有什麼危險，畢竟，學校裡都是像我這樣的學生。

　　請原諒我接下來要說的話。我知道要你們放手很難，但是這是我的人生。我想要更多挑戰，以及學習如克服這些挑戰。請讓我住校吧！

愛你們的，
傑克

** ————————————————————

campus〔ˈkæmpəs〕*n.* 校園　　***on campus*** 在校園裡
attend〔əˈtɛnd〕*v.* 上（學）
university〔ˌjunəˈvɜsətɪ〕*n.* 大學
prefer〔prɪˈfɜ〕*v.* 比較喜歡　　reason〔ˈrizn̩〕*n.* 理由
child〔tʃaɪld〕*n.* 孩子　　graduate〔ˈgrædʒuˌet〕*v.* 畢業
legally〔ˈligl̩ɪ〕*adv.* 在法律上
independent〔ˌɪndɪˈpɛndənt〕*adj.* 獨立的
depend on 依賴　　compete〔kəmˈpit〕*v.* 競爭
in the future 未來　　risk〔rɪsk〕*n.* 危機
be full of 充滿了　　forgive〔fɚˈgɪv〕*v.* 原諒
be about to 即將　　***let go*** 放掉；放開
challenge〔ˈtʃælɪndʒ〕*n.* 挑戰
overcome〔ˌovɚˈkʌm〕*v.* 克服

83. The Advantages of Clubs

Dear Mom,

I feel really sad because you always stop me from joining any activities in my club. I know you worry about my schoolwork, and I thank you for your concern. *I appreciate that you always think of me and want the best for me.* But I really love my club, and I think it's good for me, too.

I have learned lots of things in my club. *For example,* I am better at getting along with others now. I'm also learning how to plan activities, and I am developing responsibility. *Besides all that,* it is fun and relaxing. *I think I study better after enjoying some time with my club.* I hope you understand and can change your mind.

Love,

Jack

83. 社團的優點

親愛的媽媽：

　　我眞的很傷心，因爲您總是阻止我參加社團的任何活動。我知道您擔心我的學業，我也很謝謝您這麼關心。我很感激您總是想到我，處處要給我最好的。但是我眞的很喜歡我的社團，而且我也認爲社團對我有益。

　　我在社團學到很多東西。舉例來說，我現在比較會跟別人相處了。我也正在學習如何規劃活動，培養責任感。此外，社團也很有趣，氣氛又輕鬆。我想在享受社團時光後，我的讀書效率會更好。我希望您能諒解，並改變您的心意。

愛您的，

傑克

** ————————————————

advantage〔əd'væntɪdʒ〕*n.* 優點

club〔klʌb〕*n.* 社團　　***stop sb. from V-ing*** 阻止某人~

activity〔æk'tɪvətɪ〕*n.* 活動　　worry〔'wɝɪ〕*v.* 擔心

schoolwork〔'skul,wɝk〕*n.* 課業

concern〔kən'sɝn〕*n.* 關心

appreciate〔ə'priʃɪ,et〕*v.* 感激　　***think of*** 想到

be good at 擅長　　***get along with*** 與…和睦相處

plan〔plæn〕*v.* 規劃　　develop〔dɪ'vɛləp〕*v.* 培養

responsibility〔rɪ,spɑnsə'bɪlətɪ〕*n.* 責任；責任感

besides〔bɪ'saɪdz〕*prep.* 除了…之外（還有）

relaxing〔rɪ'læksɪŋ〕*adj.* 輕鬆的

change one's mind 改變心意

84. Surfing the Net

Dear Mom and Dad,

Recently, we have had lots of arguments. I have been playing too many computer games and spending too much time surfing the Net. I know that you both just want me to study hard. *I shouldn't be wasting all my time on the Net.* But I hope you can trust me. I'm not a child anymore, and I can control my time well.

In fact, before you talked to me about this thing, I had already made a plan to change my habits. I will divide my time between studying and playing. I promise that I will pay more attention to my academic performance and won't make you worry about me. *I will spare no efforts to be the first in my class to prove my determination.*

I hope you can loosen the limit you have put on my Net surfing if I reach my goal. I really don't want to be a burden on you, so I will work hard to succeed.

Sincerely,

Annie

84. 上網的問題

親愛的爸媽：

　　最近我們常常爭吵。我一直玩太多電玩遊戲，並且花太多時間上網。我知道你們只是要我用功讀書。我不應該浪費所有的時間來上網。但是我希望你們能信任我，我已經不是小孩了，我可以好好控制自己的時間。

　　事實上，在你們跟我談論這件事之前，我已經打算要改變我的習慣。我會劃分出讀書和玩樂的時間。我保證，我會更注意自己在學業方面的表現，不會讓你們擔心。我會很努力成為班上的第一名，以證明我的決心。

　　如果我達成目標，希望你們能放鬆對我上網的限制。我真的不想成為你們的負擔，所以我會努力追求成功。

安妮　敬上

** ──────

Net surfing 上網　　recently〔ˈrisn̩tlɪ〕*adv.* 最近
argument〔ˈɑrgjəmənt〕*n.* 爭論　　surf〔sɝf〕*v.* 上（網）
the Net 網際網路（= *the Internet* = *the Web*）
not…anymore 不再…　　divide〔dəˈvaɪd〕*v.* 劃分
promise〔ˈprɑmɪs〕*v.* 保證　　attention〔əˈtɛnʃən〕*n.* 注意力
pay more attention to 更注意
academic〔ˌækəˈdɛmɪk〕*adj.* 學術的
performance〔pɚˈfɔrməns〕*n.* 表現
spare〔spɛr〕*v.* 吝惜　　*spare no efforts* 不遺餘力
determination〔dɪˌtɝməˈneʃən〕*n.* 決心
loosen〔ˈlusn̩〕*v.* 放寬；放鬆　　*put limit on* 限制
goal〔gol〕*n.* 目標　　burden〔ˈbɝdn̩〕*n.* 負擔

85. A Study Tour in the U.S.

Dear Mom,

As you know, my school sponsors a 30-day study trip in the U.S. I have asked permission to join the tour before, but you said no. I understand and respect your wishes. *However*, this year I think it would be very beneficial for me to take this trip.

I have three good reasons why you should let me go. *Number one*, it would improve my English skills. This is important for the college entrance exam. Only the students with good English get accepted to the top schools. *Number two*, it would broaden my horizons. It would be good for me to meet people from other cultures. The experience of going abroad cannot be replaced by books and films. *You need to go, do, and see for yourself*. Haven't you always told me this?

And finally, number three, it would teach me to be independent. *I am very eager to show that I am capable of taking care of myself*. From the bottom of my heart, I wish to join the study tour. Would you please reconsider your position? That is all I ask. Just give it another thought. Maybe you can sleep on it?

Love,
Jane

85. 去美國遊學

親愛的媽媽：

　　您知道我的學校要贊助一趟三十天的美國遊學團，我之前有問過您可不可以參加，但是您說不行，我了解而且也尊重您的意願。但是，我覺得今年參加這個行程能讓我獲益良多。

　　我有三個為什麼您應該讓我去的很好的理由。第一，遊學可以改善我的英文能力，這對大學入學考試來說是很重要的，只有英文好的學生才能進入頂尖的學校。第二，遊學也可以拓展我的眼界。能認識來自其他文化的人對我是有益的。書本以及電影無法取代實際出國的經驗。你必須親自到那裡，去親身體驗，以及親眼見證，這難道不是您常對我說的嗎？

　　最後，第三，遊學能教導我獨立自主。我很渴望讓大家知道我能夠照顧自己。我打從心底想參加這次的遊學。能請您重新考慮您的立場嗎？這就是我想請求的，請您再想想。或許您可以睡醒再做決定嗎？

愛您的，
珍

** ──────────

sponsor〔'spɑnsɚ〕*v.* 贊助　　***study trip*** 遊學團
permission〔pɚ'mɪʃən〕*n.* 允許　　wish〔wɪʃ〕*n.* 希望；意願
beneficial〔,bɛnə'fɪʃəl〕*adj.* 有益的
broaden* one's *horizons 拓展眼界　　replace〔rɪ'ples〕*v.* 取代
***for* oneself** 親自　　independent〔,ɪndɪ'pɛndənt〕*adj.* 獨立的
eager〔'igɚ〕*adj.* 渴望的　　capable〔'kepəbl̩〕*adj.* 有能力的
take care of 照顧　　***from the bottom of*** one's *heart* 打從心底
reconsider〔,rikən'sɪdɚ〕*v.* 重新考慮
position〔pə'zɪʃən〕*n.* 立場　　thought〔θɔt〕*n.* 思考；考慮
sleep on it 睡醒再做決定

86. Asking for Permission

Dear Mom and Dad,

I am now a second-year high school student. It is likely that this year might be my last chance to attend the Count Down concert. Next year, I will be studying for the college entrance exam. *There won't be an opportunity like this again.*

Therefore, I'd like to join my friends and have fun for the last time. After the concert, I will go to a friend's house for a barbecue. Her parents agreed that we can stay overnight. Please don't worry, we are all girls. There won't be any boys with us. *We will have parental supervision at all times.* My friend's parents will bring me back the next morning.

I really want to have fun with my friends on the last day of the year. I won't have any time for fun in my third year. Please allow me to do this. I promise to work harder next year and do my best in everything.

Sincerely,

Barbie

86. 請求允許

親愛的爸爸媽媽：

　　我現在高中二年級，今年可能是我參加跨年倒數演唱會最後一次的機會，明年我就要唸書準備大學入學考試，將不會再有像這樣的機會了。

　　因此，我想和我的朋友一起玩最後一次。演唱會結束後，我們會去一個朋友家烤肉。她的父母同意我們住在她們家。請不要擔心，我們都是女孩子，沒有男生同行。我朋友的父母會隨時照顧監督我們，他們隔天還會送我回家。

　　我真的很想在一年的最後一天跟朋友們玩。升上高三之後，我將不再有時間玩樂。請你們准許我去跨年。我答應你們，我明年將會更努力，把每件事都盡力做到最好。

芭比　敬上

**

permission〔pə'mɪʃən〕n. 允許
likely〔'laɪklɪ〕adj. 可能的　　attend〔ə'tɛnd〕v. 參加
the Count Down concert 跨年倒數演唱會
college entrance exam 大學入學考試
opportunity〔ˌɑpə'tjunətɪ〕n. 機會
join〔dʒɔɪn〕n. 加入；和～一起做同樣的事
have fun 玩得愉快　　barbecue〔'bɑrbɪˌkju〕n. 烤肉
stay overnight 過夜　　parental〔pə'rɛntḷ〕adj. 父母的
supervision〔ˌsupə'vɪʒən〕n. 監督　　*at all times* 隨時
allow〔ə'lau〕v. 允許　　promise〔'prɑmɪs〕v. 保證
do one's best 盡力

87. A Letter to a Vendor

To Whom It May Concern:

I have browsed the designs of T-shirts on your website. I would like to order some T-shirts for my junior high school class. *However*, I have quite a few questions.

First, is there a discount for large orders? I will need approximately 50 shirts. Could you tell me how many shirts we must purchase in order to get a discount? *Also*, do you offer any free services, such as monogramming, for large orders? *Second*, how much is shipping? Is the fee waived on larger orders? Or does your company have a retail shop? If it isn't too far from my school, maybe I could pick them up. *Third*, I want to know whether we can exchange or return any unused T-shirts. *Last but not least*, would it be possible to see a sample? The pictures on your website are good; *however*, I would like to feel the fabric.

After receiving your replying, I will make a decision. Thanks for reading my e-mail. Please reply as soon as you can. *I'm looking forward to doing business with you*.

Sincerely,

Mark Chen

87. 給賣方的一封信

敬啓者：

　　我已經瀏覽過你們網站的 T 恤的設計，我想替我的國中班級訂購一些 T 恤，但是，我有相當多的問題。

　　第一，大批訂購有折扣嗎？我大概需要五十件。可以告訴我，我們必須購買多少件襯衫才會有折扣嗎？此外，大批訂購你們有提供像是繡字母組合圖案的免費服務嗎？第二，運費要多少錢？大批訂購可以不要算運費嗎？還是你們有零售店，如果離我的學校不遠，或許我可以過去拿貨。第三，我想知道可不可以更換或是退還沒穿過的 T 恤。最後一項要點是，我能看看樣品嗎？你們網站上的照片看起來很不錯，但是我想摸摸看布料。

　　收到你們的回覆後，我就會做決定。謝謝你們看我的電子郵件，請儘快回覆，我很期待能跟你們交易。

　　　　　　　　　　　　　　　　　　陳馬克　敬上

** ───────────

vendor〔'vɛndɚ〕*n.* 賣主；小販　　browse〔brauz〕*v.* 瀏覽
website〔'wɛb,saɪt〕*n.* 網站　　***quite a few*** 相當多
discount〔'dɪskaunt〕*n.* 折扣
approximately〔ə'prɑksəmɪtlɪ〕*adv.* 大約
purchase〔'pɝtʃəs〕*v.* 購買
monogram〔'mɑnə,græm〕*v.* 繡組合文字圖案
shipping〔'ʃɪpɪŋ〕*n.* 運費　　fee〔fi〕*n.* 費用
waive〔wev〕*v.* 撤銷　　retail〔'ritel〕*adj.* 零售的
pick up 拿取　　exchange〔ɪks'tʃendʒ〕*v.* 更換
last but not least 最後一項要點是
sample〔'sæmpl̩〕*n.* 樣品　　feel〔fil〕*v.* 摸摸看
fabric〔'fæbrɪk〕*n.* 布料　　***look forward to*** 期待

88. Working Holiday

To Whom It May Concern:

I am interested in spending some time in your country on a working holiday. I am a citizen of Taiwan and I am a student at one of my country's best universities. *I hope to gain more experience of the world and improve my English skills by spending several months in Australia.*

I have a few questions. *My first question* is about the minimum academic requirement. Is it necessary to have completed a bachelor's degree? Or are current university students eligible for the program? *Second*, are there employment agencies to help me with locating a suitable job? *Third*, I would like to begin my working holiday next March. When should I begin the application process?

Thank you for reading my questions, and I am looking forward to your reply.

Sincerely yours,
Joe Chen

88. 打工度假

敬啓者：

　　我對到貴國打工度假有興趣。我是台灣公民，就讀於台灣一所優秀的大學。我希望能獲得更多有關這個世界的經驗，並透過待在澳洲幾個月來改善我的英語能力。

　　我有一些問題。第一是關於最低學歷的要求。必須要完成學士學位嗎？還是目前在就讀大學的學生也符合資格呢？第二，有沒有職業介紹所能幫我找到合適的工作呢？第三，我明年三月想要開始打工度假，應該什麼時候開始申請呢？

　　謝謝您看我的問題，我很期待您的回覆。

陳喬　敬上

** ————————————————

working holiday 打工度假　　citizen (ˈsɪtəzn̩) *n.* 公民
gain (gen) *v.* 獲得　　improve (ɪmˈpruv) *v.* 改善
minimum (ˈmɪnəməm) *adj.* 最低限度的
academic (ˌækəˈdɛmɪk) *adj.* 學術的
requirement (rɪˈkwaɪrmənt) *n.* 要求
complete (kəmˈplit) *v.* 完成
bachelor's degree 學士學位　　current (ˈkɜənt) *adj.* 目前的
eligible (ˈɛlɪdʒəbl̩) *adj.* 合格的
program (ˈprogræm) *n.* 方案；計劃
employment (ɪmˈplɔɪmənt) *n.* 雇用
agency (ˈedʒənsɪ) *n.* 代辦處　　locate (loˈket) *v.* 找到
suitable (ˈsutəbl̩) *adj.* 適合的
application (ˌæpləˈkeʃən) *n.* 申請　　***look forward to*** 期待
reply (rɪˈplaɪ) *n.* 回答

89. Requesting Financial Assistance

Dear Principal Chen,

My name is Bill. I represent the music club. We have a bit of a problem. We are hoping you might be able to help us. As you know, the music club holds an annual concert and party. *However,* this year, we don't have enough money to cover the expense. This is not due to misuse of funds. It's actually because our budget was slashed by the school administration.

As you also know, this party serves two main purposes. *First,* it lets us show off what we have learned in the music club. *It gives the members a sense of achievement to perform at this event. Second,* the party is a charity fundraiser. Friends and family are encouraged to buy tickets. It is always held at the Silver Oak Orphanage, and all proceeds are donated to the kids.

We are not asking for much. We need a small outlay of funds to cover expenses. Certainly, you wouldn't want to disappoint the children of the orphanage. We really need your help.

Your student,

Bill Lee

89. 要求金援

親愛的陳校長：

　　我的名字是比爾，我是音樂社的代表。我們目前遇到一點小問題，我們希望您或許可以幫助我們。您知道的，音樂社每年都會舉辦年度音樂會以及派對，但是今年我們的錢不足以支付這些費用。這並不是因為資金運用不當，其實是因為我們的預算被學校行政單位刪減了。

　　您也知道，我們的派對有兩個目的。第一是要展現我們在音樂社所學，這能給在這個活動演出的社員一種成就感。第二，這個派對也是一場慈善募款活動。朋友及家人都被鼓勵購票入場。辦派對的地點一直都在銀橡樹孤兒院，所有募得的款項也都會捐贈給那裡的小孩。

　　我們要求的並不多，只需要一小筆經費來負擔支出。相信您一定不想讓孤兒院裡的孩子們失望。我們真的需要您的幫助。

您的學生，
李比爾

**　*　—

request〔rɪˋkwɛst〕v. 要求　　financial〔fəˋnænʃəl〕adj. 財務的
assistance〔əˋsɪstəns〕n. 協助　　represent〔ˏrɛprɪˋzɛnt〕v. 代表
annual〔ˋænjʊəl〕adj. 一年一度的　　cover〔ˋkʌvɚ〕v. 支付
expense〔ɪkˋspɛns〕n. 支出　　***due to*** 由於
misuse〔mɪsˋjus〕n. 誤用　　fund〔fʌnd〕n. 資金
actually〔ˋæktʃʊəlɪ〕adv. 事實上　　budget〔ˋbʌdʒɪt〕n. 預算
slash〔ˋslæʃ〕v. 刪減
administration〔ədˏmɪnəˋstreʃən〕n. 行政部門
serve〔sɝv〕n. 符合（目的）　　***show off*** 炫耀；展露
a sense of achievement 成就感　　charity〔ˋtʃærətɪ〕n. 慈善
fundraiser〔ˋfʌndˏrezɚ〕n. 募款會
orphanage〔ˋɔrfənɪdʒ〕n. 孤兒院　　proceeds〔ˋprosidz〕n. pl. 收益
donate〔ˋdonet〕v. 捐贈　　outlay〔ˋaʊtˏle〕n. 經費

90. Regretfully Declining an Invitation

Dear Albert,

Thanks for inviting me to your Christmas party. I was so excited when I received the invitation. Everyone is looking forward to the holiday. *What a joyous time for people.* Unfortunately, I will not be able to attend. Please allow me to explain.

My father has always been important to me. As you may know, he has been working overseas. *Therefore,* I haven't seen him for a couple of years. We finally received the good news that he will be returning home soon. During the holiday season we will be holding several family reunions. Everyone is truly excited to see him after such a long time. *Of course,* you understand how important family is, and this reunion is made even more special around the holiday season.

I hope you can accept my apology. *I really wish I could attend the party this time.* Please do remember to invite me next year!

Sincerely yours,

George

90. 很遺憾地回絕邀請

親愛的亞伯特：

　　謝謝你邀請我參加你的聖誕派對，我收到邀請函的時候很興奮。每個人都很期待這個節日，這是大家都覺得歡樂的時刻。遺憾的是，我不能來參加，請聽我解釋。

　　我父親一直以來都對我很重要，你知道他一直都在國外工作，所以我已經好幾年沒見到他了。後來我們收到他很快就要回家的好消息。聖誕假期期間，我們會舉辦多場家庭聚會，在這麼久的一段時間之後，大家對於能見到他都很興奮。當然你也了解家人有多麼重要，而且這次家庭聚會因為是在聖誕假期，所以更顯得特別。

　　我希望你能接受我的道歉。我真的很希望能參加這次的派對。請記得明年一定要邀請我！

喬治　敬上

** ─────────────

regretfully〔rɪ'grɛtfəlɪ〕*adv.* 遺憾地

decline〔dɪ'klaɪn〕*v.* 拒絕

invitation〔͵ɪnvə'teʃən〕*n.* 邀請；邀請函

look forward to 期待　　joyous〔'dʒɔɪəs〕*adj.* 歡樂的

unfortunately〔ʌn'fɔrtʃənɪtlɪ〕*adv.* 不幸地；遺憾地

attend〔ə'tɛnd〕*v.* 參加　　allow〔ə'laʊ〕允許

explain〔ɪk'splen〕*v.* 解釋

overseas〔'ovɚ'siz〕*adv.* 在國外　　***a couple of*** 幾個

holiday season 休假期（聖誕節、復活節、八月等）

hold〔hold〕*v.* 舉辦　　reunion〔rɪ'junjən〕*n.* 重聚；團圓

apology〔ə'palədʒɪ〕*n.* 道歉

91. A Missed Love Connection

Dear Handsome Boy,

I don't know your name, but we see each other every day. We pass each other at the bus stop. I'm the girl with the long brown hair. I always have a flower in my hair. You are the boy with the handsome smile and purple shoes. You're always eating your breakfast at the bus stop. Here's another clue. You always wear a red jacket and a blue hat when you go to play basketball.

I'm writing this because I really want to talk to you. *However*, I feel awkward starting a conversation. I wish you would just walk up to me and start talking. That would make everything a lot easier. It's obvious that I like you. *You're so handsome that I can't take my eyes off you*. I really want to know you better.

Maybe next time you see me, you will approach me. Don't be nervous. I won't bite! *Let's give it a shot*. You won't be disappointed.

Sincerely yours,

May

91. 錯過的愛情

帥氣的男孩你好：

　　我不知道你的名字，但是我們每天都見面，我們總在公車站牌前擦身而過。我是留棕色長髮的女孩，頭上總是別著一朵花。你是有著帥氣笑容，穿紫色鞋子的男孩，你總是在公車站吃早餐。另一個線索就是，你去打籃球的時候，總是穿著紅色外套，並戴著一頂藍色帽子。

　　我寫這封信是因為我真的很想跟你說話，但是我覺得要開口先跟你攀談很尷尬，我希望你能過來跟我說話，那樣的話，事情就簡單多了。顯然我很喜歡你。你很帥，讓我的目光無法移開，我真的很想要更認識你。

　　或許下次你再見到我的時候，你會接近我。不要緊張，我不會咬人！試試看吧，你不會失望的。

梅　敬上

**

pass〔pæs〕v. 經過　**bus stop** 公車站
clue〔klu〕n. 線索
awkward〔'ɔkwəd〕adj. 不自在的；尷尬的
walk up to 走向　obvious〔'ɑbvɪəs〕adj. 明顯的
take one's **eyes off** 將目光從…上面移開
approach〔ə'protʃ〕v. 接近
nervous〔'nɝvəs〕adj. 緊張的
give it a shot 試試看 (= give it a try)
disappointed〔ˌdɪsə'pɔɪntɪd〕adj. 失望的

92. A Letter to an Advice Columnist

Dear Lady Vivian,

My name is Jane and I'm a senior high school student. *Recently*, there has been a problem that really makes me feel anxious and depressed. I can't deal with the schoolwork and my club activities at the same time. I'm a member of the string club in my school, and we need to practice after school every day. Sometimes we stay at school to practice until nine o'clock p.m. When I get home, I am too tired to study anymore.

My school performance is getting worse, but I don't want to quit the string club. I love the string club very much on account of our sincere friendship and the happy times we have. *Furthermore*, I have learned so much that I couldn't gain in ordinary classes. *What can I do?* How can I find a balance between my schoolwork and the string club? *Would you give me some advice, please?*

Sincerely yours,

Jane

92. 寫給爲讀者提供建議的專欄作家

親愛的薇薇安小姐：

　　我叫作珍，我是高中生。最近有一個問題一直讓我感到非常焦慮跟沮喪，我沒有辦法同時兼顧學校課業與社團活動。我在學校是弦樂社的成員，我們每天放學後都得練習。有時我們會待在學校，練習到晚上九點，回到家就累到沒辦法唸書。

　　我的學業每況愈下，可是我並不想要放棄弦樂社。由於我們誠摯的友誼以及擁有的快樂時光，我非常喜愛弦樂社。此外，我還學到很多一般學校課程沒有的東西。我該怎麼辦？我該如何在學校課業與弦樂社之間取得平衡？能請妳給我一些建議嗎？

珍　敬上

**

columnist〔'kɑləmnɪst〕*n.* 專欄作家
anxious〔'æŋkʃəs〕*adj.* 焦慮的
depressed〔dɪ'prɛst〕*adj.* 沮喪的　　***deal with*** 應付；處理
schoolwork〔'skul,wɜk〕*n.* 課業
club〔klʌb〕*n.* 社團　　string〔strɪŋ〕*n.*（樂器）弦
performance〔pə'fɔrməns〕*n.* 表現
quit〔kwɪt〕*v.* 放棄　　***on account of*** 因爲；由於
sincere〔sɪn'sɪr〕*adj.* 眞誠的　　gain〔gen〕*v.* 獲得
ordinary〔'ɔrdn̩,ɛrɪ〕*adj.* 普通的
balance〔'bæləns〕*n.* 平衡
advice〔əd'vaɪs〕*n.* 勸告；建議

93. A Letter of Regret

Dear Mr. Gardener,

　　I am writing on behalf of XYEL in regard to our financial support of Andrew Orphanage. We here at XYEL recognize the value of your organization in our society. We have felt honored to offer what support we could over the years. *Unfortunately*, our company has suffered in the latest financial crisis and is about to close. *As a result*, our cooperation with the orphanage will also have to come to an end.

　　We all feel extremely sorry about the situation. Our employees have made a collection of their own money to help tide you over until you can find alternative funding. *A check is enclosed in this letter*. We all hope that it will help. We know that you will put it to good use as always. We are all grateful for the good work of Andrew Orphanage and hope that your operations will not be disrupted by this change.

　　　　　　　　　　　　Sincerely,
　　　　　　　　　　　　Susan

93. 一封表示遺憾的信

親愛的加德納先生：

我謹代表 XYEL 公司寫這封信，要向您通知關於我們對安德魯孤兒院的財務資助的問題。我們 XYEL 公司十分認同貴機構在我們社會上的價值。這些年來，能盡力資助貴機構，我們深感榮幸。遺憾的是，敝公司因為最近的一波金融危機而遭受損失，即將要結束營業。因此，我們與孤兒院的合作也必須結束。

對於這樣的情況，我們都覺得非常遺憾。我們的員工已經發動募捐，想要幫助你們度過難關，直到你們找到別人資助為止。隨函附寄一張支票。我們都希望能幫上忙。我們知道，你們會和往常一樣，善用這筆錢。我們都很感激安德魯孤兒院的善行，希望你們的運作不會因為這樣的改變而中斷。

蘇珊 敬上

** ————————————————————

regret〔rɪˋgrɛt〕*n.* 後悔；遺憾　*on behalf of* 代表
in regard to 關於　　financial〔fəˋnænʃəl〕*adj.* 財務的；金融的
support〔səˋport〕*n.* 支持；援助
orphanage〔ˋɔrfənɪdʒ〕*n.* 孤兒院
recognize〔ˋrɛkəgˌnaɪz〕*v.* 承認；認可
suffer〔ˋsʌfɚ〕*v.* 蒙受損失　　crisis〔ˋkraɪsɪs〕*n.* 危機
close〔kloz〕*v.* 停止營業　　cooperation〔koˌɑpəˋreʃən〕*n.* 合作
come to an end 結束　　extremely〔ɪkˋstrimlɪ〕*adv.* 非常地
employee〔ˌɛmplɔɪˋi〕*n.* 員工　　collection〔kəˋlɛkʃən〕*n.* 募捐
tide sb. over 使某人度過（困難時期）
alternative〔ɔlˋtɜnətɪv〕*adj.* 代替的；另一可供選擇的
fund〔fʌnd〕*v.* 資助　　enclose〔ɪnˋkloz〕*v.*（隨函）附寄
put…to good use 善用　　*as always* 和往常一樣
grateful〔ˋgretfəl〕*adj.* 感激的　　operation〔ˌɑpəˋreʃən〕*n.* 運作
disrupt〔dɪsˋrʌpt〕*v.* 使混亂；使中斷

94. Planning Ahead for Mom's Birthday

Dear Barbie,

How have you been lately, sis? As you know, next Sunday is Mom's 50th birthday. I want to talk about how to celebrate this big day for her. It's such a turning point in life, so I want to give her a surprise. *Actually,* I have already made a plan.

First, I want you to call Mom and tell her that you have a lot of work to do and that you won't be able to come home on her birthday. Of course, she will be disappointed. *Then,* I will call all her old friends. We'll invite them over for the big day. *Mom will definitely be excited to see her bosom friends show up.* *Next,* there is the issue of a gift. I have already bought a pearl necklace. It's the one which she saw one year ago in a magazine. You can give me your half of the money when you get home.

The only problem now is dinner. Do you think it better for us to stay at home or dine out? After all, there will be a lot of people.

Please write back as soon as possible. I want to make sure I have enough time to deal with the dinner issue. *Have a good day!*

Love,
Jill

94. 事先規劃媽媽的生日

親愛的芭比：

　　姊，最近過得還好嗎？妳你知道下個星期天是媽媽五十歲生日，我想跟妳討論要怎麼替媽媽慶祝這個大日子。這是人生的一個轉捩點，所以我想給她一個驚喜。其實，我已經擬定了一個計劃。

　　首先，我想要妳打給媽媽，告訴她妳有很多工作要做，沒辦法在她生日那天回家。當然，媽媽會很失望。然後，我會打給她所有的老朋友，我們邀請他們來慶祝這個大日子，媽媽看到她的好朋友出現一定會很高興。接下來是禮物的問題，我已經買了一條珍珠項鍊，妳知道就是一年前媽媽在雜誌上看到的那個，妳可以到家時再給我妳那一半的錢。

　　最後，現在唯一的問題就是晚餐，妳覺得我們要待在家裡吃，還是外出用餐好呢？畢竟，我們會有很多人。

　　請儘快回信，我想要確定我有足夠的時間搞定晚餐的問題。祝妳順心！

愛妳的妹妹，
吉兒

**

ahead〔əˋhɛd〕*adv.* 事先　　***How have you been?*** 你好嗎？
lately〔ˋletlɪ〕*adv.* 最近　　sis〔sɪs〕*n.* 姊妹（= *sister*）
celebrate〔ˋsɛləˏbret〕*v.* 慶祝　　***turning point*** 轉捩點
actually〔ˋæktʃʊəlɪ〕*adv.* 事實上
disappointed〔ˏdɪsəˋpɔɪntɪd〕*adj.* 失望的
definitely〔ˋdɛfənɪtlɪ〕*adv.* 一定
bosom〔ˋbuzəm〕*adj.* 親密的；心腹的　　***bosom friend*** 密友
show up 出現　　pearl〔pɝl〕*n.* 珍珠
necklace〔ˋnɛklɪs〕*n.* 項鍊　　issue〔ˋɪʃu〕*n.* 問題
dine out 在外面吃飯　　***deal with*** 應付；處理

95. I'm Innocent

Dear X17,

　　Recently, I got the news that I was fined because you took a picture of me supposedly littering. *In fact*, I was not littering. What your photo showed was very misleading. It is true that I threw a piece of paper, but I threw it toward a trash can. *Unfortunately*, I missed and didn't realize it. If I had, I would have turned around and picked it up. *In that situation*, I think it was obvious that I did not litter on purpose.

　　I wish you would have simply told me about my mistake instead of trying to make money off of it. *I am sorry that I made a mistake, but you should be sorrier*. I don't believe that you really care about improving the society. I think you only care about making a profit. *You should be ashamed of yourself*.

Sincerely,

Jill Lee

95. 我是無辜的

親愛的 X17：

　　最近，我得知我被罰款，是因爲你拍了一張疑似我亂丟垃圾的照片。事實上，我並沒有在亂丟垃圾。你的照片很容易引起誤解。我眞的丟了一張紙，但是我是把它丟進垃圾桶。不巧，我沒丟中，而且並不知情。如果我當時知道的話，就會轉頭把那張紙撿起來。在那樣的情況下，我想很明顯我並不是故意亂丟垃圾。

　　我希望當時你能告訴我，而不是靠這個來賺錢。我很抱歉我犯了錯，但是你比我更該抱歉。我不相信你是眞的在乎要改善這個社會，我想你在乎的只是能不能賺錢。你應該要爲你的行爲感到羞愧。

李吉兒　敬上

**　————————————————

innocent〔ˈɪnəsn̩t〕*adj.* 無辜的
recently〔ˈrisn̩tlɪ〕*adv.* 最近　　fine〔faɪn〕*v.* 罰款
supposedly〔səˈpozdlɪ〕*adv.* 根據推測；據說
litter〔ˈlɪtɚ〕*v.* 亂丟垃圾
misleading〔mɪsˈlidɪŋ〕*adj.* 誤導人的　　***trash can*** 垃圾筒
unfortunately〔ʌnˈfɔrtʃənɪtlɪ〕*adv.* 不幸地；遺憾地
realize〔ˈriəˌlaɪz〕*v.* 了解　　***pick up*** 撿起來
obvious〔ˈɑbvɪəs〕*adj.* 明顯的　　litter〔ˈlɪtɚ〕*v.* 亂丟垃圾
on purpose 故意地　　***care about*** 關心
improve〔ɪmˈpruv〕*v.* 改善　　profit〔ˈprɑfɪt〕*n.* 利潤
make a profit 獲利
ashamed〔əˈʃemd〕*adj.* 感到慚愧的
be ashamed of 對…感到慚愧

96. **The Bachelorette Party**

Dear Barbie,

I was totally surprised to receive the wedding invitation! I couldn't believe my eyes. I read the letter again and again. Barbie is getting married! Congratulations!

I do believe you'll be happy with Ken. He is kind and friendly. *Of course*, I will attend the wedding. *However*, I also want to hold a "bachelorette party" for you. After the ceremony, you will be Ken's wife. You won't be able to go to a pub at night. You won't be able to drink wine with your friends. You won't be able to go out all the time. *So, I want to give you an opportunity to do something crazy before you tie the knot.*

Let me tell you my plan. *First*, I will call our old senior high school friends. We can have a party in a karaoke room. We can yell, laugh and do whatever we want to do! At the end of the party, I'll give you a present. Give me some time to prepare the party. You won't regret. Just look forward to it! Congratulations again!

Sincerely,

Jill

96. 單身派對

親愛的芭比：

　　收到妳的喜帖我真的很驚訝！我無法相信我的眼睛。那張喜帖我看了又看。芭比真的要結婚了！恭喜！

　　我真的相信妳跟肯在一起會幸福的。他善良又友善。當然，我一定會去參加婚禮，但是我也想先替妳辦一場「單身派對」。婚禮過後，妳就是肯的老婆，晚上就不能去酒吧，妳就沒有辦法跟朋友喝酒，或是隨時出門了。所以我想在妳結婚之前，給妳機會做一些瘋狂的事。

　　我跟妳說我的計畫。首先，我會打電話給我們高中時的老朋友。我們可以在卡拉 OK 的包廂裡舉辦派對。我們可以大叫、大笑，而且想做什麼就做什麼！派對快結束時，我會送妳一份禮物。給我一些時間準備派對。妳不會後悔的。敬請期待！再次恭喜妳！

吉兒　敬上

** ───────────────

bachelorette〔͵bætʃələˈrɛt〕*n.* 未婚女子

bachelorette party 女子婚前單身派對

totally〔ˈtotḷɪ〕*adv.* 完全地　　wedding〔ˈwɛdɪŋ〕*n.* 婚禮

invitation〔͵ɪnvəˈteʃən〕*n.* 邀請函

wedding invitation 喜帖（= *wedding card*）

congratulations〔kən͵grætʃəˈleʃənz〕*n. pl.* 恭喜

attend〔əˈtɛnd〕*v.* 參加　　hold〔hold〕*v.* 舉辦

ceremony〔ˈsɛrə͵monɪ〕*n.* 典禮　　***all the time*** 隨時

opportunity〔͵ɑpəˈtjunətɪ〕*n.* 機會　　***tie the knot*** 結婚

karaoke〔͵kɑrɑˈoke〕*n.* 卡拉 OK　　yell〔jɛl〕*v.* 大叫

regret〔rɪˈgrɛt〕*v.* 後悔　　***look forward to*** 期待

97. A Plea for Help

Dear Strangers,

Help! My name is Jill, and I was kidnapped by a vicious woman—Cher. She is extremely attractive. She has exotic eyes that burn with fire, a delicate nose, and the most unbearable, fragile look. *Her beauty is beyond anyone's imagination.* If you see her, be careful! *It is almost impossible to resist her charm!* She uses it to lure unsuspecting children away from home. Then she sells them to parents who don't have kids!

Tomorrow is my judgment day. I will be sold to another family. *However,* if things don't go smoothly — if they don't like me or they won't pay enough — she will kill me! The place they have appointed for the trade is on Clearwater Avenue at the corner of River Lane. Kind strangers, I beg you to bring the police to that place and rescue me!

Desperately,

Jill

97. 請求救援

陌生人你好：

　　救命！我叫吉兒，我被一個叫雪兒的惡毒女人綁架了。她長得很好看，有一雙充滿異國風情、像火焰燃燒般的大眼、精緻的鼻子，和令人無法抗拒、纖弱的表情。她美到超出任何人的想像。如果你見到她，千萬要小心！要抗拒她的魅力，幾乎是不可能的！她利用這樣的美貌來誘拐天眞的小孩離家，然後再把這些小孩賣給沒有孩子的父母！

　　明天就是我的最後審判日了。我要被賣到另一個家庭。不過，如果交易進行得不順利——如果買主不喜歡我，或是錢付得不夠——這個女人就會殺了我！她們指定的交易地點在克里爾沃特路靠近立佛巷的轉角。好心的陌生人，我求你們帶警察到那個地方救我！

情況危急的，

吉兒

---

plea〔pli〕*n.* 懇求　　**kidnap**〔'kɪdnæp〕*v.* 綁架

vicious〔'vɪʃəs〕*adj.* 惡毒的　　**extremely**〔ɪk'strimlɪ〕*adv.* 非常地

attractive〔ə'træktɪv〕*adj.* 吸引人的

exotic〔ɪg'zɑtɪk〕*adj.* 有異國風味的　　**delicate**〔'dɛləkət〕*adj.* 精緻的

unbearable〔ʌn'bɛrəbl̩〕*adj.* 忍不住的；令人難以忍受的

fragile〔'frædʒəl〕*adj.* 纖弱的　　**look**〔lʊk〕*n.* 表情

resist〔rɪ'zɪst〕*v.* 抗拒　　**charm**〔tʃɑrm〕*n.* 魅力

judgment day 最後審判日；世界末日　　**lure**〔lʊr〕*v.* 引誘

unsuspecting〔͵ʌnsə'spɛktɪŋ〕*adj.* 不懷疑的

smoothly〔'smuðlɪ〕*adv.* 順利地　　**appoint**〔ə'pɔɪnt〕*v.* 指定

avenue〔'ævə͵nju〕*n.* 大道　　**lane**〔len〕*n.* 巷子

rescue〔'rɛskju〕*v.* 拯救

desperately〔'dɛspərɪtlɪ〕*adv.* 情況緊急地

98. A Letter to a Teacher

Dear Mr. Lin,

I am very upset that you accused me of cheating. My parents have always taught me to have integrity. *For me, doing my own work is a matter of principle.* Yesterday, I spent about two hours on the assignment. Although I was exhausted, my mom encouraged me to finish it. Her encouragement gave me the strength to finish it by myself.

When I heard that you said I had copied someone else's homework, and deducted five points, I was in shock. Mr. Lin, I can assure you that I did not copy my assignment. Virtue is my most valuable asset. I regard copying others' homework to be the worst thing that I could do. Although I know that if I took the easy way out, I would have more free time, I still refuse to do it because my integrity is more important.

I really hope you will investigate this matter. *Also,* you can call my mom to ask if the content of this letter is true. *I really looking forward to having my name cleared.*

Sincerely,

Phil

98. 給老師的一封信

親愛的林老師：

　　我對您指控我作弊這件事很難過。我父母一直教導我要正直。對我來說，把自己的事做好是原則問題。昨天，我花了兩小時寫作業，雖然很累，但是我媽媽還是鼓勵我把它完成。她的鼓勵給我力量獨自完成。

　　當我聽到您說我抄襲別人的作業，因而扣了我五分時，我很震驚。林老師，我可以跟您保證，我沒有抄襲別人的作業。品行是我最珍貴的特質，我認為抄襲別人的作業是最糟糕的事。雖然我知道，如果我用簡易的辦法，就會有更多空閒時間，但是我還是不會這樣，因為正直更重要。

　　我真的希望您能調查一下這件事。另外，您也可以打電話問我媽媽這封信的內容是不是真的。我真的很期待能洗刷我的污名。

菲爾　敬上

** ——————————————————

upset〔ʌpˋsɛt〕*adj.* 難過的；生氣的　　accuse〔əˋkjuz〕*v.* 指控
cheat〔tʃit〕*v.* 作弊　　integrity〔ınˋtɛgrətı〕*n.* 正直
principle〔ˋprınsəpl〕*n.* 原則　　assignment〔əˋsaımənt〕*n.* 作業
exhausted〔ıgˋzɔstıd〕*adj.* 筋疲力盡的
encourage〔ınˋkɜıdʒ〕*v.* 鼓勵　　strength〔strɛθ〕*n.* 力量
copy〔ˋkɑpı〕*v.* 抄寫　　deduct〔dıˋdʌkt〕*v.* 扣除
point〔pɔınt〕*n.* 分　　shock〔ʃɑk〕*n.* 震驚
assure〔əˋʃur〕*v.* 向～保證　　virtue〔ˋvɜtʃu〕*n.* 美德
asset〔ˋæsɛt〕*n.* 資產　　regard〔rıˋgɑrd〕*v.* 認為
way out 擺脫困境的辦法；出路
investigate〔ınˋvɛstə‚get〕*v.* 調查
content〔ˋkɑntɛnt〕*n.* 內容　　*look forward to* 期待
name〔nem〕*n.* 名聲　　clear〔klır〕*v.* 去除…的污點

99. A Postcard from Taiwan

Dear Father,

Today is our first day in Taipei. It's hard to describe everything we saw. Taipei 101, the highest building in Taiwan, was under my feet! Although we didn't go all the way to the top, the view from the sixty-fourth floor was still marvelous.

The second place we visited in Taipei was the Grand Hotel. *It looks just like a toy when you see it from far away.* Up close, it is an incredible building. The Chinese architecture was stunning. *You can't imagine how awe-inspiring it was!* After the Grand Hotel, it was dinnertime. We went to Shilin Night Market. Although it was crowded, we had fun. And all of the food was delicious.

Although we only went to three places, the first day in Taipei was great. I'm excited about tomorrow. We will visit the National Palace Museum.

Your loving son,

Andy

99. 來自台灣的明信片

親愛的爸爸：

今天是我們在台北的第一天。很難描述我們所看到的一切。台北 101，台灣最高的大樓，就在我的腳下！雖然我們沒有一路上到最高的地方，但是從六十四樓看出去的景色依舊很棒。

我們在台北的第二站是圓山大飯店。從很遠的地方，它看起來就像一個玩具。靠近一看，它是一座雄偉的建築。中式建築風格令人嘆為觀止，你無法想像它是多麼令人肅然起敬！參觀完圓山飯店後，晚餐時間到了。我們來到士林夜市，雖然很擁擠，但是很好玩，而且東西都很好吃。

雖然我們只去了三個地方，台北的第一天真的很棒。我很期待明天，我們要去故宮博物院。

愛你的兒子，
安迪

** ————————————

postcard (ˈpostˌkɑrd) *n.* 明信片　　describe (dɪˈskraɪb) *v.* 描述
all the way 一路　　view (vju) *n.* 景色
floor (flor) *n.* 樓層　　marvelous (ˈmɑrvḷəs) *adj.* 很棒的
the Grand Hotel 圓山大飯店　　***from far away*** 從遠方
up close 靠近　　incredible (ɪnˈkrɛdəbḷ) *adj.* 令人無法相信的
architecture (ˈɑrkəˌtɛktʃɚ) *n.* 建築
stunning (ˈstʌnɪŋ) *adj.* 驚人的　　imagine (ɪˈmædʒɪn) *n.* 想像
awe (ɔ) *v.* 敬畏　　inspire (ɪnˈspaɪr) *v.* 激發
awe-inspiring (ˈɔɪnˌspaɪərɪŋ) *adj.* 令人肅然起敬的
Shilin Night Market 士林夜市　　crowded (ˈkraʊdɪd) *adj.* 擁擠的
the National Palace Museum 國立故宮博物院
loving (ˈlʌvɪŋ) *adj.* 充滿著愛的

100. A Letter Asking for Advice

Dear Ms. Cheer,

I have a big problem, *and I hope that you can help me*. My best friend has started taking drugs and I am very worried. I don't know what to do.

I have tried my best to persuade him to stop doing it. I told him that it was against the law and that it's dangerously addictive and enormously expensive. I also reminded him of the long-term harm to his health. But he won't listen to me. He thinks he can control it. *Of course*, he can't, and now I'm afraid that he is addicted. I feel so much regret that I couldn't change his mind before it was too late.

Now, I'm thinking about turning him in even if it might put him in jail. But if I do that, not only might I might lose this friend forever, but I might also ruin his chances to have a good future. *I can't make up my mind what to do*. *Would you please advise me?*

Sincerely,

Phil

100. 一封請求建議的信

親愛的琪兒女士：

　　我有一個嚴重的問題，希望妳能幫忙。我最好的朋友開始吸毒，我非常擔心，我不知道該如何是好。

　　我已盡力勸阻他停止吸毒，我告訴他這是違法的，會有上癮的危險，而且非常昂貴。我也提醒他，吸毒會對健康帶來長期的傷害。可是他不聽我的話，他認為他可以控制。當然，他無法自制，現在恐怕已經上癮了，我很後悔沒有及時改變他的想法。

　　現在我想舉發他，即便他有可能吃牢飯。但是如果我這麼做，我不僅可能永遠失去這個朋友，也可能毀掉他未來的前途！我不知該如何是好，可以請妳給我一些建議嗎？

菲爾　敬上

**

advice〔əd'vaɪs〕*n.* 忠告；建議　　**take drugs** 吸毒
worried〔'wɝɪd〕*adj.* 擔心的
persuade〔pɚ'swed〕*v.* 說服　　**against the law** 違法的
addictive〔ə'dɪktɪv〕*adj.* 使人上癮的
enormously〔ɪ'nɔrməslɪ〕*adv.* 非常地；巨大地
remind〔rɪ'maɪnd〕*v.* 提醒
long-term〔'lɔŋ,tɝm〕*adj.* 長期的
addicted〔ə'dɪktɪd〕*adj.* 上癮的
turn in 舉發　　**put sb. in jail** 使某人入獄
ruin〔'ruɪn〕*v.* 破壞；毀掉
make up sb's mind 下定決心　　advise〔əd'vaɪz〕*v.* 建議

附 錄

【84 年學測】

說明： 依提示在「答案卷」上寫一封 100 至 150 字的信。評分標準：內容 5 分，
組織 5 分，文法 4 分，用字拼字 4 分，體例（格式、標點、大小寫）2 分。

提示： 高中生王治平收到美國筆友 George 的來信，告訴治平他要隨父母到
台灣來住兩年左右，並問治平："Can you give me some advice and
suggestions so that I know what I should do and what I should not do
when I am in Taiwan?" 現在請你以治平的身份，擬一封適當的回信給
George，歡迎他來台灣，並且針對他的問題，提出一些具體的建議。

Advice on Living in Taiwan

Dear George, February 20, 1995

I'm really glad to hear that you're coming to Taiwan.
During your stay here, you must make good use of the two
years to see Taiwan for yourself. Taiwan, as you already know,
is a mountainous island. *Therefore*, the first thing you should
do is pay a visit to our scenic mountains, such as Mt. Ali and Mt.
Jade. *You will be deeply impressed with the grandeur and
magnificence of the mountains*. When you have had enough
of the gorgeous scenery, try the food at the local night market.
The tasty snacks will make you want one more bite.

But beware of the traffic in big cities. You should avoid
the rush hours lest you get stuck in the heavy traffic. When you
go downtown, take the bus if possible. If you drive, you may
find it hard to park. When you stroll along the sidewalk, watch
out for the motorcycles parked on it. The traffic in Taiwan is
quite different from that in the States. *Finally*, I'm going to say,
"Welcome to Taiwan." *I'm sure you'll find it interesting to
live in Taiwan*.

Your friend,
Chih-ping

關於定居台灣的建議

1995 年 2 月 20 日

親愛的喬治：

　　很高興得知你要來台灣。在台灣定居的時候，你得好好利用這兩年，親自看看台灣。如你所知，台灣是一個多山的島嶼，所以你第一件該做的事，就是去遊覽我們風景優美的群山，像是阿里山和玉山。你一定會對這些高山的雄偉和壯麗印象深刻。在飽覽了美麗的景緻之後，試試在地的夜市美食。美味的小吃一定會讓你想要再嚐一口。

　　但是，你要留意大都市裡的交通。你應該避開尖峰時段，免得被困在車陣中。出門去市中心時，盡量搭公車。如果開車的話，你會發現很難停車。當你漫步在人行道上的時候，小心停在上面的摩托車。台灣的交通跟美國的大不相同。最後，我想跟你說：「歡迎你來台灣。」我相信你一定會覺得住在台灣很有趣。

你的朋友，
治平

**
stay〔ste〕*n.* 停留期間　　***make good use of*** 好好利用
for *oneself* 親自　　mountainous〔ˋmaʊntn̩əs〕*adj.* 多山的
pay a visit to 參觀；拜訪
be deeply impressed with 對～印象深刻
scenic〔ˋsinɪk〕*adj.* 風景優美的　　grandeur〔ˋgrændʒɚ〕*n.* 雄偉
magnificence〔mægˋnɪfəsn̩s〕*n.* 壯麗
gorgeous〔ˋgɔrdʒəs〕*adj.* 很漂亮的　　***night market*** 夜市
tasty〔ˋtestɪ〕*adj.* 好吃的　　snack〔snæk〕*n.* 小吃
bite〔baɪt〕*n.* 一口　　***beware of*** 小心
rush hours 尖峰時間　　lest〔lɛst〕*conj.* 以免
get stuck in 被困在～中　　park〔pɑrk〕*v.* 停車
stroll〔strol〕*v.* 漫步

【94 年指考】

說明: 1. 依提示在「答案卷」上寫一篇英文作文。
2. 文長至少 120 個單詞。

提示: 指定科目考試完畢後,高中同學決定召開畢業後的第一次同學會,你被公推負責主辦。請將你打算籌辦的活動寫成一篇短文。文分兩段,第一段詳細介紹同學會的時間、地點及活動內容,第二段則說明採取這種活動方式的理由。

An Activity for Graduates

July 2, 2005

Dear Fellow Graduates,

Now that the college entrance exam is over, we are about to begin a brand-new and exciting stage in our lives. *However*, it is important to remember the past and keep in touch with those who have made our high school years special. *Therefore*, we have organized a picnic for all the graduates. In addition to a barbecue, there will be games and a singing contest. The event will take place on Sunday, July 17, at Yangmingshan Park. Buses will leave the school at 11:00 am and return at 5:00 pm.

I hope that all graduates will attend, for this may be our last chance to spend some time together. During the activity we may share our memories of high school and our plans for the future. *Most importantly*, it is a chance for us to end our high school careers on a positive note by relaxing and having fun after enduring the stress of the entrance exam.

Sincerely,

Mary

畢業生同學會

2005 年 7 月 2 日

親愛的畢業生：

　　既然大學入學考試結束了，我們也即將展開人生中一個嶄新且令人興奮的階段。但是緬懷過往，以及與讓我們的高中生活如此特別的同學們保持聯繫，也是很重要的。所以我們替所有的畢業生舉辦了一場野餐。除了烤肉以外，我們也會進行一些遊戲以及舉辦歌唱大賽。活動將於七月十七日，星期天，在陽明山公園舉辦。接駁公車將於早上十一點從學校出發，下午五點回來。

　　我希望所有的畢業生都能參加，因為這或許是我們最後一次能相聚的機會。在活動期間，我們可以分享高中時的回憶，以及對未來的計劃。最重要的是，這場活動能讓我們在承受過大考的壓力之後放鬆享樂一下，為高中生活畫下完美的句點。

瑪麗　敬上

**

graduate〔'grædʒuɪt〕n. 畢業生　　*now that* 既然；由於
college entrance exam 大學入學考試　　*be about to* 即將
brand-new〔'brænd'nju〕adj. 嶄新的　　stage〔stedʒ〕n. 階段
keep in touch 保持聯絡　　organize〔'ɔrgən,aɪz〕v. 舉辦
in addition to 除了～以外（還有）
barbecue〔'barbɪ,kju〕n. 烤肉會　　contest〔'kantɛst〕n. 比賽
event〔ɪ'vɛnt〕n. 大型活動　　*take place* 舉行
attend〔ə'tɛnd〕v. 參加　　career〔kə'rɪr〕n. 生涯
positive〔'pazətɪv〕n. 正面的　　note〔not〕n. 特徵；氣氛
on a…note 以一種…的氣氛　　endure〔ɪn'djur〕v. 忍受
stress〔strɛs〕n. 壓力

【97 年學測】

說明：1. 依提示在「答案卷」上寫一篇英文作文。
　　　2. 文長 120 個單詞（words）左右。

提示：你（英文名字必須假設為 George 或 Mary）向朋友（英文名字必須假設為 Adam 或 Eve）借了一件相當珍貴的物品，但不慎遺失，一時又買不到替代品。請寫一封信，第一段說明物品遺失的經過，第二段則表達歉意並提出可能的解決方案。**請注意**：為避免評分困擾，請使用上述提示的 George 或 Mary 在信末署名，<u>不得使用自己真實的中文或英文姓名</u>。

An Apology Letter

Dear Eve,　　　　　　　　　　February 2, 2008

　　I'll be honest with you. I lost your digital camera at the concert last night. I promised I'd be extra careful with it, and I was. *However*, there were so many people yesterday, and the crowd got out of hand. When I was taking pictures, people kept bumping into me. The camera fell out of my hand, and there wasn't even space to bend down, let alone look for it. I stayed after the concert and searched, but to no avail.

　　Please forgive me. You don't know how sorry I am. *I know you had precious pictures in there, not to mention the camera itself.* I definitely will pay for a new camera. Just give me some time. And to compensate for the pictures and memories, let me take to wherever you want. *Again, I'm truly sorry for what happened, and hope that I can make it up to you.*

　　　　　　　　　　　　　　　　Sincerely,
　　　　　　　　　　　　　　　　George

道 歉 信

2008 年 2 月 2 日

親愛的夏娃：

　　我要跟妳坦白一件事。我昨晚去演唱會時，弄丟了妳的數位相機。我保證過，我會特別小心保管妳的相機，而我也的確如此。不過，昨天的人太多了，群衆變得難以控制。當我在拍照時，大家一直撞到我。相機從我手中掉落，而且當時沒有空間可彎下腰，更別提去尋找了。我在演唱會結束後留下來找，但卻徒勞無功。

　　請原諒我。妳不知道我有多抱歉。我知道妳有珍貴的相片在裡面，更別提相機本身了。我一定會付錢買一台新相機。只要給我一點時間。而且爲了要彌補那些照片和回憶，讓我帶妳去任何妳想去的地方吧。我要再次眞誠地爲所發生的事表示歉意，並且希望我可以彌補妳。

喬治　敬上

**

digital camera　數位相機

concert〔'kɑnsɝt〕*n.* 音樂會；演唱會

promise〔'prɑmɪs〕*v.* 保證　　extra〔'ɛkstrə〕*adv.* 額外地

get out of hand　失控　　*bump into*　撞上

bend down　彎腰　　*let alone*　更別提

search〔sɝtʃ〕*v.* 搜尋　　*to no avail*　無效

forgive〔fɚ'gɪv〕*v.* 原諒

precious〔'prɛʃəs〕*adj.* 珍貴的　　*not to mention*　更別提

definitely〔'dɛfənɪtlɪ〕*adv.* 必定

compensate〔'kɑmpən,set〕*v.* 彌補

make it up to sb.　彌補某人

【101 年學測】

說明： 1. 依提示在「答案卷」上寫一篇英文作文。

2. 文長約 100 至 120 個單詞（words）。

提示： 你最好的朋友最近迷上電玩，因此常常熬夜，疏忽課業，並受到父母的責罵。你（英文名字必須假設為 Jack 或 Jill）打算寫一封信給他/她（英文名字必須假設為 Ken 或 Barbie），適當地給予勸告。**請注意**：必須使用上述的 Jack 或 Jill 在信末署名，不得使用自己的真實中文或英文名字。

Advice to a Friend About a Bad Habit

Dear Ken,   Jan. 18, 2012

You know that I always support you but you've been spending far too much time playing video games—and suffering the consequences as a result. *Of course*, I love video games too and I understand how easy it is to get wrapped up in them. *However*, when the games begin to have an effect on your education and relationships, something has to give.

Moderation is the key to everything and video games are no exception. I'm not saying you should stop playing video games altogether but I am strongly suggesting you cut back a little, if for no other reason than to keep your parents off your back. You could try my method, which is to set a limit of two hours per day. I think you'll come to realize that life will be much easier when your parents aren't constantly scolding you. *And besides*, you really don't want to mess up your future, do you? *Anyway, if there's anything I can do to help you, don't hesitate to ask.*

Your friend,

Jack

規勸朋友戒除壞習慣的信

2012 年 1 月 18 日

親愛的肯：

你知道我一直都是支持你的，但是你花太多時間打電玩了，也因此承受了後果。當然，我也愛電玩，而我也了解，迷上電玩是很容易的事。然而，當電玩開始影響你的教育和人際關係，就必須有所改變。

任何事情都要適度，這是要訣，而電玩也不例外。我並不是說你應該完全停止打電玩，但是我強烈建議你應該稍微減少一點，不為別的，這樣至少可以讓你的父母不要再煩你。你應該試試我的方法，那就是每天限定玩兩小時。我覺得你會開始了解到，當你的父母不再一直責備你，生活就會過得輕鬆許多。此外，你真的不會想要搞砸你的未來，是吧？無論如何，如果有什麼我可以幫你的，不要猶豫，儘管開口。

你的摯友
傑克

**

video game 電玩遊戲　suffer〔'sʌfə〕 *v.* 遭受
consequence〔'kɑnsə,kwɛns〕 *n.* 後果　*as a result* 因此
get wrapped up 沉迷　*have an effect on* 對～有影響
Something has to give. 必須有所改變。
moderation〔,mɑde'reʃən〕 *n.* 適度
key〔ki〕 *n.* 關鍵　exception〔ɪk'sɛpʃən〕 *n.* 例外
altogether〔,ɔltə'gɛðə〕 *adv.* 徹底地
cut back 減量　*keep sb. off your back* 讓某人不再煩你
constantly〔'kɑnstəntlɪ〕 *adv.* 不斷地
scold〔skold〕 *v.* 責罵　*mess up* 搞砸
hesitate〔'hɛzə,tet〕 *v.* 猶豫

心 得 筆 記 欄

劉毅英文家教班成績優異同學獎學金排行榜

姓 名	學 校	總金額	姓 名	學 校	總金額	姓 名	學 校	總金額
謝家綺	板橋高中	40600	蘇紀如	北一女中	11100	林建宏	成功高中	6300
王芊蓁	北一女中	36850	陳怡靜	北一女中	11000	江婉盈	中山女中	6100
吳書軒	成功高中	36100	謝承孝	大同高中	10900	林柏翰	中正高中	6000
趙啓鈞	松山高中	34650	陳亭如	北一女中	10400	徐詩婷	松山高中	5900
袁妤蓁	武陵高中	32850	鄭涴心	板橋高中	10100	吳宇珊	景美女中	5800
林怡廷	清華大學	27800	何思瑩	和平高中	10000	洪珮榕	板橋高中	5700
王挺之	建國中學	27200	遲定鴻	格致高中	9400	吳秉學	師大附中	5700
羅之勵	大直高中	25900	黃靖儒	建國中學	9300	蔡承絍	景美女中	5600
蕭允惟	景美女中	25500	陳冠儒	大同高中	9200	王凱弘	師大附中	5600
黃筱雅	北一女中	25000	徐子瑤	松山高中	9000	翁子惇	縣格致中學	5500
王廷鎧	建國中學	24400	吳易倫	板橋高中	9000	許廷瑋	延平高中	5400
許嘉容	北 市 商	24400	潘育誠	成功高中	8800	林原道	和平高中	5400
潘羽薇	丹鳳高中	19600	陳庭偉	板橋高中	8800	陳子文	成功高中	5400
蘇芳萱	大同高中	19500	王千瑀	景美女中	8700	陳姿穎	縣格致中學	5400
林政穎	中崙高中	18800	巫冠毅	板橋高中	8600	謝承諭	建國中學	5300
郭學豪	和平高中	18700	黃新雅	松山高中	8600	戚世旻	格致高中	5300
邱瀞葦	縣格致中學	18300	林承慶	建國中學	8600	謝孟儒	百齡高中	5300
郭子瑄	新店高中	17500	謝竣宇	建國中學	8400	簡君恬	師大附中	5100
柯博軒	成功高中	17500	江 方	中山女中	8300	施昊恩	板橋高中	5000
陳瑾慧	北一女中	16500	吳念馨	永平高中	8200	周湘承	時雨國中	5000
陳聖妮	中山女中	16400	王舒亭	縣格致中學	8200	周書廷	明倫高中	4900
蔡欣儒	百齡高中	16300	潘威霖	建國中學	8100	謝育姍	景美女中	4800
施衍廷	成功高中	15700	吳沛璉	靜修女中	7900	呂昀靜	縣格致中學	4700
詹皓翔	新莊高中	15500	俞欣妍	大直高中	7900	林宇嫻	板橋高中	4700
廖彥綸	師大附中	15400	林妤靜	格致高中	7800	林珈欣	格致高中	4700
何俊毅	師大附中	14800	楊沐焓	師大附中	7750	杜懿樺	新莊高中	4600
陳 昕	麗山高中	14600	許瑞庭	內湖高中	7700	孫廷瑋	成功高中	4600
簡士益	格致高中	14500	高維均	麗山高中	7700	徐銘聰	明德高中	4500
宋才聞	成功高中	14500	李承祐	成功高中	7700	林禹辰	成功高中	4400
王秉立	板橋高中	14300	吳蜜妮	西松高中	7700	黃紹瑋	格致高中	4400
廖崇鈞	大同高中	13800	林冠宏	林口高中	7600	鄭倢安	中山女中	4300
鄭 晴	北一女中	13800	鄭懿珊	北一女中	7600	楊葰蓁	格致高中	4300
張馥雅	北一女中	13700	林育汝	中山女中	7400	朱品潔	內湖高中	4300
方冠予	北一女中	13500	柯賢鴻	松山高中	7400	盧姿樺	育成高中	4200
范詠琪	中山女中	13400	張譽馨	板橋高中	7300	張瑀倩	明倫高中	4200
吳思慧	景美女中	13300	陳冠廷	薇閣國小	7150	陳建豪	格致高中	4200
許瓊中	北一女中	13100	謝瑜容	中山女中	7100	羅勻彤	北一女中	4100
溫哲興	延平高中	12200	郭禹溱	北一女中	7000	林天佑	中崙高中	4100
應奇穎	建國中學	12000	詹 羽	師大附中	6900	林庭瑜	新莊高中	4100
劉楫坤	松山高中	11900	游宗憲	竹林高中	6800	陳建良	格致高中	4100
廖芃軒	武陵高中	11800	張繼元	華江高中	6600	許庭軒	靜修女中	4000
盧昱瑋	格致高中	11550	張長蓉	薇閣高中	6500	李文淵	西松高中	4000
呂濬瑝	成功高中	11400	蘇瑢瑄	景美女中	6400			
陳宣蓉	中山女中	11200	黃崇愷	成功高中	6400			

※ 因版面有限，尚有領取高額獎學金
同學，無法列出。

劉毅英文教育機構
台北本部：台北市許昌街17號6F（捷運M8出口對面・學善補習班）　　TEL：(02) 2389-5212
台中總部：台中市三民路三段125號7F（光南文具批發樓上・劉毅補習班）　TEL：(04) 2221-8861
www.learnschool.com.tw

高中書信英作文 100 篇

主　　編 / 劉　毅

發　行　所 / 學習出版有限公司　☎ (02) 2704-5525

郵　撥　帳　號 / 05127272 學習出版社帳戶

登　記　證 / 局版台業 *2179* 號

印　刷　所 / 裕強彩色印刷有限公司

台 北 門 市 / 台北市許昌街 10 號 2 F　☎ (02) 2331-4060

台灣總經銷 / 紅螞蟻圖書有限公司　☎ (02) 2795-3656

本公司網址　www.learnbook.com.tw

電 子 郵 件　learnbook@learnbook.com.tw

售價：新台幣一百八十元正

2016 年 1 月 1 日新修訂

ISBN 978-986-231-172-1